T0243515

The
CHOSEN.

BOOK FOUR

BroadStreet Publishing® Group, LLC
Savage, Minnesota, USA
BroadStreetPublishing.com

THE CHOSEN. Book Four: 40 Days with Jesus

9781424563906 (faux leather)
9781424563913 (e-book)

Represented by Steve Laube with the Steve Laube Agency

Design and typesetting by Garborg Design Works | garborgdesign.com
Editorial services by Michelle Winger | literallyprecise.com

Printed in Malaysia.

23 24 25 26 27 5 4 3 2 1

The
CHOSEN

BOOK FOUR

BroadStreet

PUBLISHING

TABLE OF CONTENTS

FOREWORD

The first verse actually happened.
The second verse mostly happened,
and the third verse, of course, is happening now.

- Bruce Springsteen, "Greatest Hits" liner notes

Twenty years ago I wrote a song in the midst of a dark season of life. I had been recently diagnosed with Hepatitis C (I was infected through a blood transfusion when I was a child) and had begun a form of immune suppressing therapy. I had lost forty pounds and was anemic. Every Friday (for almost two years) I knew I would be sick.

Starting several years prior, I had been attending a Bible study that basically was going through the narrative story of the Scriptures. We learned about the context in which the events of Scripture happened, namely the culture and history of the people in the Bible as well as the geography of the land. Starting in Genesis, the Bible study leader talked about the way in which the God of Abraham, Isaac, and Jacob revealed Himself. In particular, the story of Jacob—a man, not perfect but having a certain level of tenacity, who was willing to wrestle with God through the night—stood out. As I heard this story, my imagination filled in the setting. But that story made room for mine. After all, it is my humble assertion that great art not only tells the story of the artist, but it somehow (more so) makes room for the person taking it in.

It was in that environment I started writing worship music. Two years later, that song was "Your Grace Is Enough."

It was the process of seeing the narrative story of the Scriptures come alive in the different dimensions of culture, time, geography, and history—of old promises being foretold in the new—that created space and sparked my imagination as a songwriter. The process of reading the Scriptures and imagining oneself in the story is an old practice known as *lectio divina*. Not just in the reading of Scripture but in the daily context of a life lived in relationship with God, we are in the story.

You realize over time that history is often repeating itself, and the story of sinners being made into saints by the all-consuming grace and love of Jesus is something that is still unfolding. He is truly reconciling all things to Himself.

Even our imaginations. Even in our art.

Devoting picture, sound, and light toward spending tens of hours to see the New Testament in such a specific way through The Chosen™ gives dimension to cultural, historical, and spiritual context. That is something we as the Body of Christ have never had in this scope. We also now have the capacity to watch it simultaneously; it is truly an amazing gift.

Who knows where inspiration will strike as we go on this journey together. What other people will be inspired by this show? I know my imagination and my faith have been encouraged by it. But you know what still holds immeasurable value? Do you know what it doesn't replace? An actual relationship with Jesus! Which means, we commit to a journey of faith with Scripture, prayer, and resources that help us with that journey, such as this devotional.

Like the story of Emmaus in the Gospel of Luke, Jesus often shows up "on the way," while we are walking, while we are living, even in our disappointment and grieving, as Day 34 tells us, for example. There's a process in which our eyes are opened as the Scriptures are unpacked. Sometimes a pilgrimage of faith can be a season; for some it can be years. But the practice of embracing a defined period of time to pursue God and to be receptive to His pursuit of us is something that every follower of Jesus has to keep entering into as we dive deeper and deeper into this story of all stories.

That's the heart behind this book. It's an opportunity to enter into forty days of walking with Jesus intentionally. If you can commit to the journey, He commits to showing up and revealing Himself. God willing, we too shall say, "Were our hearts not burning within us?" Your heart, after all, is what the Lord wants. I pray this devotional helps you in your surrender of it.

Matt Maher

INTRODUCTION

Jesus came to fulfill Scripture (Luke 4:21). That's what He said after reading from the scroll of Isaiah in His hometown synagogue. Everyone was impressed until He rebuked them for their unbelief. Then they were furious and tried to throw Him off a cliff.

Jesus came to seek and save the lost (Luke 19:9). That's what He said after instructing Zacchaeus to climb down from the tree so they could hang out at his house. The elated tax-collector swiftly repented and vowed to change his crooked ways.

Jesus came to testify to the truth (John 18:37). That's what He said after being questioned by Pilate about His identity and alleged crimes. Moments before handing Him over to be crucified, Pilate rhetorically asked, "What is truth?" (John 18:38)

The literal answer? *Jesus is truth*. He is the way, the truth, and the life. And no one comes to the Father except through Him (John 14:6). Which begs the question:

What is our response to truth? Which side of it are we on? As it happens, Jesus said, "Everyone on the side of truth listens to me" (John 18:37).

Here's the thing about truth though: We contend with it in a variety of ways under a variety of circumstances (as evidenced by these three examples). Once Jesus collides with our deepest needs, cultural biases, personal motivations, and prideful objections, the outcome can be infuriating. Or exhilarating. Or anything in between.

Here's another thing about truth: it can take a minute to grasp. Zaccheaus had already heard about Jesus before climbing the tree for a better look. Mercifully, Jesus repeated Himself often and illustrated Kingdom principles again and again. Which means if anyone missed it the first time, they had plenty more opportunities to understand.

If they were listening.

We're far enough in our journey together that many of the stories we discuss will be familiar and may even seem repetitive—because some of them are. And as you read through this book, you might find yourself wondering, *Didn't they already do a devotional (or three) on this verse…or person, or miracle, or principle, or promise?* Maybe we have. And that's ok since—as Jesus and the four gospel accounts make pretty clear—we learn through repetition, and truth sometimes takes a minute to grasp.

To that end, we invite you to climb up and continue to explore all the angles from which we can better see Jesus. Let's spend the next forty days listening harder as we contend with the answers given by our Scripture-fulfilling, lost-seeking-and-saving, truth-testifying Messiah.

May we welcome His rebuke.

May we repent of our crooked ways.

Then may we testify to the Truth who is ever working within us…the outcome of which should be nothing short of exhilarating.

Amanda, Kristen, and Dallas

VERY GREAT REWARD

"Beware of practicing your righteousness before
other people in order to be seen by them,
for then you will have no reward
from your Father who is in heaven."

MATTHEW 6:1

Jesus warned the sermon-on-the-mount folks not to practice their righteousness before others in order to be seen. Moments later He said, "Let your light shine before others, so that they may see your good works and give glory to your Father who is in heaven" (Matthew 5:16).

The being seen part wasn't the issue because recognition

is not inherently bad. Stealing God's glory instead of shining for Him is where it gets dark, and the consequences are real.

Nonetheless, most of us have a difficult time staying focused on God's rewards because they're just not as immediate and tangible as we'd like them to be. So, even though "no eye has seen, nor ear heard, nor the heart of man imagined, what God has prepared for those who love him" (1 Corinthians 2:9), we tend to prefer what we *can* imagine. And curate. And edit.

We know what eyes like to see and what ears like to hear, so we prepare all kinds of stuff for those who might love us. Then we post it and wait to hear the words: "Well done, you cool and awesome person."

Needless to say, that's about as eternal-reward forfeiting as it gets, and why every person with a social media account—or pulse—ought to heed Jesus' warning. On a fairly regular basis we need to ask ourselves: for whom do I strive to shine?

Abraham's answer earned him the moniker "father of faith." That's how shiny he was. Even after God promised to make him into a great nation (which catapulted "being seen" way beyond what any heart could imagine), Abraham's righteousness-practicing was for the sake of glorifying God. He wasn't perfect by any stretch, but he knew for whom he strove to shine. When he was promised the heir that would launch his great nation status, God said, "Do not be afraid, Abram. I am your shield, your very great reward" (Genesis 15:1 NIV).

Compare that to the glory-stealers whom Jesus told the

sermon-on-the-mount folks not to emulate. They didn't get squat. "So when you give to the needy, do not announce it with trumpets, as the hypocrites do in the synagogues and on the streets, to be honored by others. Truly I tell you, they have received their reward in full. But when you give to the needy, do not let your left hand know what your right hand is doing, so that your giving may be in secret. Then your Father, who sees what is done in secret, will reward you" (Matthew 6:2-4 NIV).

Thank goodness God's reward is not man's fleeting and meaningless admiration. It's His love and power being displayed in and through our lives for others to see. As we shine for Him, our Father who is in heaven will forever be our shield. His very great reward will carry us into eternity where He has prepared the unimaginable. And we'll finally hear the words, "Well done, good and faithful servant" (Matthew 25:21).

How cool and awesome that will be!

PRAYER FOCUS

Thank God that He loves us enough to warn us and instruct us. Ask Him to reveal the ways in which you steal His glory. Praise Him for the very great reward of His love and power working in and through your life.

MOVING FORWARD

o Do you have a difficult time staying focused on God's rewards? What immediate and tangible things tend to get in the way?

o For whom do you strive to shine most of the time? As in, are your good works for God's glory or for your own recognition?

o Describe a time when others saw your good works and gave glory to God?

WAITING FOR ALL THE THINGS

"Seek first the kingdom of God and his righteousness, and all these things will be added to you."

MATTHEW 6:33

If you read through Lamentations—which is an entire book dedicated to the crushing grief brought on by Israel's rebellion and Jerusalem's consequent fall—you'll notice a shift in the middle of the third chapter. It's quite dramatic. Shortly after penning tragic prose such as, "Like a lion in hiding, [God] dragged me from the path and mangled me" (Lamentations 3:10-11 NIV), the prophet Jeremiah remembered: "The Lord is good to those whose hope is in him, to the one who seeks him; it is good to wait quietly for the salvation of the Lord" (vv. 25-26 NIV).

Yes, it is good to wait on God. *And* it's often extremely difficult, as the grieving mangled prophet testified. Moses was another prophet who was no stranger to waiting. In his one-and-only psalm, he made an interesting comment about the Lord's timing. "A thousand years in [God's] sight are like a day that has just gone by, or like a watch in the night" (Psalm 90:4 NIV).

It's doubtful Moses could relate. Many of his days must've felt like a thousand years as he wandered around the wilderness with a bunch of whiny idolatrous ingrates. In the same psalm, he pleaded with God to expedite the process. "Relent, Lord! How long will it be? Have compassion on your servants. Satisfy us in the morning with your unfailing love, that we may sing for joy and be glad all our days" (vv. 13-14 NIV).

Smack dab in the middle of affliction, while dealing with ridiculously selfish people, both prophets knew to wait on the Lord. He was their only hope. Nearly a thousand years apart from each other, they sought the God who orchestrates millenniums and individual days simultaneously. And as promised, He was good to them. Despite their harrowing circumstances, Jeremiah and Moses were satisfied by the Lord's unfailing love.

Many centuries later when the early church was being mocked by a different group of rebellious ingrates, Peter told the believers to recall the holy prophets. He quoted Moses then extolled the Lord's goodness and compassionate timing.

"But do not forget this one thing, dear friends: With the Lord a day is like a thousand years, and a thousand years are like a day. The Lord is not slow in keeping his promise, as some understand slowness. Instead he is patient with you, not wanting anyone to perish, but everyone to come to repentance" (2 Peter 3:8-9 NIV).

Which means we're not the only ones waiting. Nor have we been the only ones seeking. Jesus said to the repentant, tree-climbing, tax collector Zacchaeus, "Today salvation has come to this house. For the Son of Man came to seek and to save the lost" (Luke 19:9-10 NIV).

That is what He's been doing for millennia. Jesus is the salvation of the Lord for whom Jeremiah quietly waited. He is the lost-seeking, patient, promise-keeping Savior who invites each person to seek Him back and experience His kingdom and righteousness. And since we tend to hear His voice more clearly when we're smack dab in the middle of a tragic chapter, that's often when the dramatic shift occurs. And the reason why God doesn't expedite the process. He's compassionate that way. Because He is our only hope.

Therefore, even when we feel mangled by crushing grief, or weary from wandering around with ridiculously selfish people (including ourselves), we can sing for joy and be glad all our days. In His perfect timing—like a day that has just gone by, or like a watch in the night—He will relent and add all of the things for which we've been waiting.

PRAYER FOCUS

Praise the God of compassion for His perfect timing as you wait for Him to move. Ask Him to satisfy you in the morning with His unfailing love while you continue to seek first His kingdom and righteousness. Thank Jesus for being the lost-seeking, patient, promise-keeping Savior who came to seek and save the lost.

MOVING FORWARD

o Have you ever cried out to the Lord in grief or frustration then felt a dramatic shift in your spirit? Describe the circumstances and what happened.

o When you seek first the kingdom of God and His righteousness, what are "these things" you are hoping will be added? Do you want the circumstances to change? Or do you hope to sing for joy despite the circumstances? (Both are okay.)

o With the benefit of hindsight, what is something that you can now see as God's patience versus what you once felt was His slowness?

DAY 3

WORD COUNT

When evening came, many who were
demon-possessed were brought to him,
and he drove out the spirits with a word
and healed all the sick.

MATTHEW 8:16 NIV

Engaging in spiritual warfare means not engaging in futile conversations. Words count. And when it comes to exercising authority over evil, less is more.

Jesus demonstrated this principle when casting out evil spirits. Since their eternal fate was sealed, there was nothing to discuss. The best a demon could hope for was temporary relocation. And even then, it ended terribly for them. On one occasion, the demons begged Jesus to be sent into a herd of pigs. Jesus said, "Go." And with a single authoritative word, the demons transferred from the two men whom they were tormenting into some nearby swine. Their clemency was short-lived, however. Seconds later, the entire herd ran down a steep bank and drowned themselves in a lake. (See Matthew 8:28-34.)

Not only was the ordeal a huge bummer for the pigs, it was straight-up terrifying for the local townsfolk. When everyone discovered what happened, they pleaded with Jesus to leave their region. Their response was understandable. That kind of authority can be enormously harmful. Which is why Jesus used most of His words to describe where His power came from and why He had it.

Jesus walked from town to town engaging in one conversation after another because, unlike the demons, people didn't know who He was or how He'd affect their eternity. Every word counted. And when it came to developing personal relationships, more was more.

His longest recorded conversation was with the Samaritan woman at the well. Per usual, it was Jesus who initiated. The woman wasn't receptive until He demonstrated His authority. But unlike the demons, pigs, and townsfolk in the other story, she wasn't terrified. The patient exchange between them resulted in the disclosure of both their identities. When Jesus declared, "I, the one speaking to you—I am [the Messiah]" (John 4:26 NIV), the woman knew where His power came from and why He had it.

Not only was the revelation a huge moment for the Samaritan woman, it was straight-up transformational for the local townsfolk. When everyone discovered what had happened, they pleaded with Jesus to stay in their region. "And because of his *words* many more became believers" (v. 41 NIV). Their response was understandable because that kind of authority can be enormously inviting.

As Christ followers we, too, have that kind of authority. We can rebuke the enemy with a single word: Go! And refuse to engage in futile conversations (internally, or otherwise). Conversely, when we share with the local townsfolk who Jesus is and who we are in Him, we triumph over the accuser by the blood of the Lamb and by the word of our testimony. (See Revelation 12:11.)

Our words count. To be Christlike means to engage in one conversation after another describing where our power comes from and why we have it. When it comes to sharing Christ, more is more because we have no idea how our words may effect someone else's eternity.

PRAYER FOCUS

Praise God for the authority you've been given over the enemy. Thank Him for your ability to rebuke evil with a single word and triumph over the accuser with the word of your testimony. Ask the Lord to embolden your speech and give you the many words to share with others who Jesus is and who you are in Him.

MOVING FORWARD

o   What does your use of words say about your walk with
    Christ?

o   Jesus used most of His words to describe where His
    power came from and why He had it. Do you do the
    same when talking about Him?

o   How has your testimony affected the people around you?

HATERS GONNA HATE

"You will be hated by everyone because of me,
but the one who stands firm to the end will be saved."

MATTHEW 10:22 NIV

In a very matter-of-fact way, Jesus was preparing His disciples for what He knew they would encounter. Hatred was part of it, but it wouldn't be the half of it. In the same send-off speech, Jesus told them to expect interrogations, floggings, arrests, and persecution. In other words, major opposition would be wholly unavoidable.

There's a reason why today's churches and non-profits have dramatically modified their Jesus pitches; it's hard to secure volunteers if flogging and arrests are mentioned. And since hatred tends to carry with it some negative connotations, it makes sense to focus instead on how good all our good works make us feel.

We are not the first generation to tweak Jesus' message. People have been trying to change His approach since He began approaching people. Even Jesus' half-brother James felt the need to offer his two-cents-worth of PR advice. He thought Jesus could use a better marketing plan.

After Jesus told the disciples to go on to Judea without Him, James said to Jesus, "'Leave Galilee and go to Judea, so that your disciples there may see the works you do. No one who wants to become a public figure acts in secret. Since you are doing these things, show yourself to the world.' For even his own brothers did not believe in him" (John 7:3-5 NIV).

In today's language, James would've stated it like this: "Jesus, you can't get famous being low-key. There's a formula. An algorithm. And you won't gain a massive crowd without following it." Objectively speaking, James wasn't entirely wrong about being seen. What invalidated his input was his lack of faith in Jesus. James forgot who he was talking to. "For even his own brother did not believe him."

Like James, we tend to try and manage Jesus. We modify His message for the sake of appealing to a broader audience. We switch tactics to gain more followers. And we work at mitigating backlash by focusing on the positive. All of which, we argue, is for the greater good.

But is it? Or are we just trying to avoid being hated?

Objectively speaking, that's not entirely wrong. No one goes around *looking* for opposition or persecution. What invalidates our argument, though, is our lack of faith in Jesus. We're forgetting who He's talking to: His disciples. The Church. Us. And we very much need to hear His matter-of-fact warning:

If we truly are on mission for Christ, major opposition is wholly unavoidable.

At some point or another, we'll likely be hated by plenty of people. But it's not our job to please the crowd by following its ways, or to focus solely on how good our good works make us feel. Our job is to proclaim the gospel and represent Jesus. That's it. And the one who stands firm to the end will be saved.

PRAYER FOCUS

Praise God that He sends us out into the world to represent Him. Ask Him for the courage to receive and endure any hatred or persecution. Thank Him for His Word that's full of matter-of-fact warnings and power-filled promises.

MOVING FORWARD

o   What kind of opposition to your faith have you encountered?

o   Has the thought of being hated caused you to modify your approach? If so, how?

o   What aspect of your faith is the most difficult to talk
    about? What response are you most afraid to receive?

YOKED
PART 1

"Come to me, all you who are weary and burdened, and I will give you rest. Take my yoke upon you and learn from me, for I am gentle and humble in heart, and you will find rest for your souls. For my yoke is easy and my burden is light."

MATTHEW 11:28-30 NIV

First things first, what's a yoke? A yoke is a wooden frame or crosspiece that fastens around the neck of a large animal tasked with carrying a heavy load. Picture a team of oxen pulling a large plow. The yoke distributes the weight evenly, making the burden easier to manage.

It's ironic that Jesus chose that imagery to relay His gentleness and humility. Almost all of the Old Testament yoke references were used to illustrate bondage and servitude. Back then, the visual was meant to solidify the nearly incomprehensible truth that the people were indeed slaves.

For example, when the Israelites were enslaved by the Babylonians, God told the prophet Jeremiah to fashion a yoke, put it around his neck, and deliver this message to a handful of influential kings: "Bow your neck under the yoke of the king of Babylon; serve him and his people and you will live" (Jeremiah 27:12 NIV).

The kings were then warned not to listen to any false prophets who spoke a different, easier message. If they did, God promised to banish them, and they would most certainly perish (v. 15).

Sure enough, a false prophet named Hananiah came along speaking a different, easier message. He boldly touted, "This is what the Lord Almighty, the God of Israel, says: 'I will break the yoke of the king of Babylon'" (28:2 NIV).

Desperate to be the hero of the story, Hananiah told the Israelites that their enslavement would soon be over. His message, of course, was nonsense, which caused Jeremiah to rebuke him for being the false-prophesying liar he was. Enraged, Hananiah broke the yoke off of Jeremiah's neck— it was all very dramatic. And then, so was the punishment because the Lord promised to remove Hananiah from the face of the earth (v. 16).

Fast forward to the folks Jesus was teaching. After years of political and religious oppression they, too, were eager for a yoke-breaking, easier message. What they received instead was the invitation to take up an easier yoke—which is a different thing altogether.

Because Jesus is the real hero of the story, only He could promise the weary and burdened people that their enslavement would soon be over. Only He could break the old yoke from their necks and replace it with the new.

Which is exactly what happened.

The perfect Son of God was fastened to a wooden frame or crosspiece and tasked with carrying the heavy load of man's sin. Picture one sinless man dying for all of humanity's disobedience. The visual solidifies the nearly incomprehensible truth that the people are indeed free. "The punishment that brought us peace was on him, and by his wounds we are healed" (Isaiah 53:5 NIV).

It's only because of the cross that we can be yoked with Christ. And the reason we can rest is because the weight has forever been distributed onto Jesus. The imagery that once represented bondage and servitude has become the means through which we may know His gentle and humble heart.

If only we come to Him.

Every last one of us will surely perish and be removed from the face of the earth. If we reject a different, easier message, and instead bow our necks under the yoke of the King of kings, we will live.

And that is how we find rest for our weary, burdened souls.

PRAYER FOCUS

Praise God for the cross and spend some time mediating on this truth: Jesus was pierced for our transgressions, He was crushed for our iniquities; the punishment that brought us peace (and rest) was upon Him, and by His wounds we are healed (Isaiah 53:5). Ask the Lord to teach you more about His gentle and humble heart. Thank Him for His easy yoke.

MOVING FORWARD

o Do you feel weary and burdened right now? How does being yoked with Jesus help ease that burden?

o Read Isaiah 53. Reflect upon all that Jesus endured to set us free and give us rest.

o What is something about Jesus that you are eager to learn and apply? Be as specific as possible.

YOKED
PART 2

"Come to me, all you who are weary and burdened, and I will give you rest. Take my yoke upon you and learn from me, for I am gentle and humble in heart, and you will find rest for your souls. For my yoke is easy and my burden is light."

MATTHEW 11:28-30 NIV

Jesus used all kinds of metaphors and parables to illustrate who He is and where He came from. But when describing what He's like (as in, His character), He summed it up with two adjectives under which everything about the Messiah could be filed:

Gentle and humble.

However, the weary and burdened Jewish people weren't

sure that was enough. They'd been waiting for a powerful political savior to crush the heavy yoke of the Roman occupation. Justice had been promised, after all. So, they were understandably confused when instead of a burst-on-the-scene-and-bring-forth-victory kind of Messiah, they got one who walked alongside them and offered rest for their souls.

Given the political climate, the unconventional-ness of it required serious faith. Which was the whole point, and why some seven hundred years earlier, the Lord gave His people a prophetic head's up. "Behold my servant, whom I uphold, my chosen, in whom my soul delights; I have put my Spirit upon him; he will bring forth justice to the nations. He will not cry aloud or lift up his voice, or make it heard in the street; a bruised reed he will not break, and a faintly burning wick he will not quench; he will faithfully bring forth justice. He will not grow faint or be discouraged till he has established justice in the earth; and the coastlands wait for his law" (Isaiah 42:1-4).

In other words, God's chosen servant never once pounded a pulpit demanding allegiance. Nor was He harsh with the confused or callous toward the broken. Instead, the humble and gentle Messiah personified the means through which justice would be established. Victory was promised to those who trusted in His name, even the Romans who enforced the oppressive occupation.

In addition to His character, the adjectives *gentle* and *humble* managed to depict His entire earthly ministry, including His death. Especially His death. "And being found in human form, he humbled himself by becoming obedient to the point of death, even death on a cross" (Philippians 2:8).

Because the heavy-yoke-crushing, rest-promising Messiah conquered the grave, the ultimate justice is assured. And so is His return. One day soon, the same Savior who didn't cry aloud or lift His voice in the street, will thunderously burst-on-the-scene and gather up His people. "For the Lord Himself will come down from heaven, with a loud command, with the voice of the archangel and with the trumpet call of God, and the dead in Christ will rise first. After that, we who are still alive and are left will be caught up together with them in the clouds to meet the Lord in the air. And so we will be with the Lord forever" (1 Thessalonians 4:16-17 NIV).

Never again will the power of Jesus' gentleness and humility be in question. Those who come to Him, take up His yoke, and learn from Him will most assuredly find rest for their once weary and burdened souls. They will walk alongside the victorious Messiah and experience forever who He is and where He came from.

PRAYER FOCUS

Praise God that everything about Jesus and His ministry could be filed under gentle and humble. Ask Him to reveal more of His character as you seek to know Him more. Thank Him for being the heavy-yoke-crushing, rest-promising Messiah you need right now.

MOVING FORWARD

o   Where is the first place you typically turn when feeling
    weary and burdened?

o   The unconventional-ness of Jesus requires faith as well
    as review. To which promises do you cling when feeling
    weary and burdened?

o   Jesus invites us to take up His light yoke and learn
    from Him. How has that changed your life? Has "rest"
    felt like a significant part of your experience?

DAY 7

BLAME GAME

"You will know the truth,
and the truth will set you free."

JOHN 8:32

Blaming someone else for our sin is way easier than accepting responsibility for it. So is blaming God. He makes for a convenient scapegoat since He created all the sinners and allows them all to sin. That was Adam's conclusion anyway. After being confronted about the whole apple-eating debacle, he decided to hedge his bets and just blame both. He said, "The woman you put here with me—she gave me some fruit from the tree, and I ate it" (Genesis 3:12 NIV).

See how easy? All culpability denied and passed to the nearest bystander. But there's a problem with making excuses instead of confessing the truth: the foolishness of it will ruin our lives and make us rage against the Lord (Proverbs 19:3).

Yikes.

Adam wasn't the only one to deceive himself with the blame game. When Moses busted Aaron for making the golden calf, Aaron's knee-jerk reaction was to pin it on the Israelites. He didn't blame God, but the story he came up with was so implausibly stupid that it would've at least sounded better if he had.

It all started when Moses was up on the mountain communing with the living God who freed the Israelites from brutal captivity. The rebellious nation grew restless while he was away and decided they needed a more immediate god. They opted for one they could see, carry around, and dance naked in front of.

Yikes.

In an attempt to evade pandemonium, Aaron told the people to give him their gold jewelry and he'd take care of the rest. "[Aaron] took what they handed him and made it into an idol cast in the shape of a calf, fashioning it with a tool" (Exodus 32:4 NIV).

Meanwhile, God instructed Moses to return to camp on account of everyone losing their minds. When he saw the golden calf, Moses was gobsmacked and implored of Aaron, "What did these people do to you, that you led them into such great sin?" (v. 21 NIV)

Aaron's answer: "Do not be angry, my lord. You know

how prone these people are to evil. They said to me, 'Make us gods who will go before us. As for this fellow Moses who brought us up out of Egypt, we don't know what has happened to him.' So I told them, 'Whoever has any gold jewelry, take it off.' Then they gave me the gold, and I threw it into the fire, and out came this calf!" (vv. 22-24 NIV)

Good grief. A four-legged statue just happened to emerge from the flames and plop itself on the ground? C'mon Aaron. And who did he say was responsible for this inexplicably random, though shockingly calf-like outcome? Everyone else. And *their* prone-ness to evil. Aaron was just trying to keep the peace.

(Even Adam was probably shaking his head at that one.)

That's how foolish deception makes us. More often than not, we're the only ones who actually believe the nonsense that comes out of our mouths. Easy as it may be, blame-shifting, excuse-making, and all the other means of denying culpability can ruin our lives because they're just big fat lies. Which means believing they'll protect us from the consequences we're seeking to avoid is implausibly stupid.

Just ask Adam.

Graciously, the same living God who created all the sinners and allows us all to sin, has also freed us from sin's brutal captivity. If we confess our prone-ness to evil and quit opting for more immediate gods, our lives won't be ruined by our own deceptive foolishness. We will know the truth and the Truth will set us free.

PRAYER FOCUS

Praise the Living God for freeing you from sin's brutal captivity. Ask Him to reveal any foolishness or self-deception in your heart. Confess the lies you've told. Thank Him for His grace and for the Truth that set you free.

MOVING FORWARD

o   Why is blame-shifting and excuse-making such a big deal? What is the root sin?

o   When was the last time you denied responsibility and blamed someone else for your sin? What was the story you told yourself or others?

o   Read through the golden calf account in Exodus 32. What was the consequence? Do you think it was too harsh? Why or why not?

THE MARK SERIES

(Who the heck is Mark?)

Not a member of the twelve apostles, Mark (a.k.a. John Mark) is the author of the second New Testament Gospel, which was probably the first one written (o/a 70 AD). He grew up in Jerusalem, and the house of his mother was a place where early Christians met (Acts 12:12).

As a young man, Mark went with his cousin, Barnabas, to Antioch. It was from there that he accompanied Barnabas and Paul on their first missionary journey to Cyprus (Acts 13:5), though he soon after deserted them and returned to Jerusalem (Acts 13:13). Paul took Silas on his second missionary journey, and Barnabas took Mark back to Cyprus (Acts 15:36-41). Perhaps due to Barnabas's mentorship, Mark eventually did work with Paul again (Colossians 4:10; 2 Timothy 4:11).

We also know Mark had a close friendship with Peter (1 Peter 5:13), and tradition tells us that his Gospel is informed by Peter's recollections.

ALL TOO FAMILIAR

[Jesus] came to his hometown, and his disciples followed
him. And on the Sabbath, he began to teach in the
synagogue, and many who heard him were astonished,
saying, "Where did this man get these things? What is the
wisdom given to him? How are such mighty works done
by his hands? Is not this the carpenter, the son of Mary
and brother of James and Joses and Judas and Simon?
And are not his sisters here with us?"
And they took offense at him.

Mark 6:1-4

They took offense at Jesus. But why?

Of all the people in the world, shouldn't Jesus' hometown
crowd have been among the first to follow Him? After all,
they had closer proximity to Him than anyone. They'd seen

the sinless Son of God grow up—no doubt they noticed He was a really good kid (1 Peter 2:21-22). They knew His father, Joseph, was in the line of David, and that the Messiah they were waiting for would be too (Isaiah 9:6-7, Matthew 1:1-16). They'd heard Jesus speak with knowledge beyond His years (Luke 2:41-47) and with authority that surpassed even the religious leaders (Matthew 7:28-29). And He was miraculously healing people (Matthew 4:23).

So, why on earth did they reject Him?

Well, because He was of the earth.

Truth is, sometimes it's hard to accept redemption stories that are born of the familiar. We prefer our heroes to come from far off places. The white knight who rides in on a noble steed. The glamorous spy and her lipstick pistol. The god of thunder or trident-carrying ruler of the sea. The bird, the plane—wait, no—that's Superman.

There's no emotional baggage with those guys.

Conversely, when stories of redemption come from imperfect, even sin-soaked places, we tend to reject them. We're wary when the jerks in our lives claim they've been saved by Jesus, because our tendency is to believe some people are irredeemable. At the same time, we're cynical when others seem "too good." We look for hypocrisy and assume moral failure is just around the bend. Maybe that's because we've seen it one too many times, or maybe it's because we've been hurt by someone who claimed to know God but really didn't.

There's just something about familiarity, about nearness

and seeing behind the curtain, that makes it difficult to believe things can change for the better. So, when Jesus' ministry emerged from the all-too familiar, people who knew Him responded poorly: "Who are *you* to tell *us* what's true? You're no different than us, no better. You're not worthy, not holy, not heroic, and you're certainly not who you're claiming to be."

Of course, Jesus was all those things and more.

Truth is, we all have varying degrees of familiarity with Jesus, the Bible, and the people who've claimed to know Him. But oh, that our experiences wouldn't get in the way of truly seeing who He is! Oh, that we'd let Jesus be the hero of our own stories, believing in His ability to miraculously save—both us and others, no matter our history. Oh, that we'd allow Him to *continue* to work in and through us because when we do, we become part of His other-worldly ministry:

To save, redeem, and heal our all-too familiar, broken world.

PRAYER FOCUS

Hold your hands open in prayer and praise Jesus as Lord. Ask God to remove any cynicism that remains toward Him or the people He has chosen. Pray for those in your life who may still be taking offense—that their hearts would be open to and accepting of the truth. And pray that you wouldn't take offense at Jesus when life doesn't go the way you want it to, and instead, that you'd continue to believe He is who He says He is.

MOVING FORWARD

o   Do you ever take offense at Jesus? In what ways are you rejecting His lordship in your life?

o   Do you ever take offense at Jesus' followers? Do you sometimes doubt His ability to redeem and restore those who may have previously rejected Him?

o   Pray through Psalm 139:23-24 and confess anything that might be hindering your faith and trust in Jesus.

FAR FAR AWAY

"This people honors me with their lips,
but their heart is far from me;
in vain do they worship me,
teaching as doctrines the commandments of men."

MARK 7:6-7

The Pharisees had taken notice of the disciples' behavior. Tradition among the Jews at that time was to wash their hands in the "proper" way. And also their cups and copper vessels and dining couches and—you get the idea.

While we can all agree that clean hands are important for good hygiene, the ceremonial washing of hands in Jesus' day was a different kind of thing. First, they had to wash off the actual dirt. Then they had to perform a ritual to make themselves spiritually clean.

44

As if a person's heart could *ever* be made clean by the washing of hands alone.

It was a man-made rule, which is why the Pharisees asked, "Why do your disciples not walk according to the tradition of the elders, but [rather] eat with defiled hands?" (v. 5) Meaning, why aren't your boys following the religious practices we've instituted that make us feel righteous, important, powerful, and spiritually clean?

Which caused Jesus to put them in their place.

"Hear me, all of you, and understand: There is nothing outside a person that by going into him can defile him, but the things that come out of a person are what defile him. For from within, out of the heart of man, come evil thoughts, sexual immorality, theft, murder, adultery, coveting, wickedness, deceit, sensuality, envy, slander, pride, foolishness. All these evil things come from within, and they defile a person" (Mark 7:14-15, 20-23).

It was a long list that had nothing to do with washing hands. As it turns out, the significance they attached to such practices became an excuse to ignore their actual sin. Indeed, the Pharisees hands were clean, and their reputations were intact, but their sin was allowed to remain because that's what religion does: it keeps our focus on outward behavior instead of our inward, desperate need for a Savior. Religion has a built-in ability to keep us far from God.

Conversely, when we draw near to God with outstretched hands and contrite hearts, when we give Him access to the things we'd prefer to hide, when we pray along with King David, "Search me, O God, and know my heart! Try me and know my thoughts! And see if there be any grievous way in me, and lead me in the way everlasting," (Psalm 139:23-24), *only then* do we escape the pitfalls of religion and enter into relationship with the Lord.

One that's based on what *He* did to make us clean.

Our hearts cannot be near to God without first becoming clean—that's true. But no amount of hand washing, penance paying, hail Mary prayers, or Sunday morning church attendance can accomplish that. Only forgiveness and salvation through Jesus can make us clean in the way that matters unto eternity.

PRAYER FOCUS

Search me, O God, and know my heart.
Try me and know my thoughts.
And see if there be any grievous way in me,
and lead me in the way everlasting.
Psalm 139:23-24

MOVING FORWARD

o   Do you spend more time worrying about having clean hands (outward behavior) or a clean heart (being right with God)?

o   What "grievous way" (i.e., sin) is the Holy Spirit
    convicting you of right now?

o   What is He encouraging you to do about it?

LEAVEN

[Jesus] cautioned them, saying, "Watch out:
beware of the leaven of the Pharisees
and the leaven of Herod."

MARK 8:15

This was a weird moment because Jesus had been performing all kinds of miracles as well as teaching and shepherding the masses—but then the Pharisees asked for sign from heaven (v. 11).

Um…you mean like all the miracles and teachings and shepherding of the masses?

No wonder Jesus "sighed deeply in his spirit" (v. 12).

The Pharisees were the religious crowd, experts in Old Testament Scripture and upstanding leaders in the community. Herod, on the other hand, was their debaucherous king who did awful, ugly things like have an affair with his sister-in-law, before lusting after her daughter, and then gifting them both with John the Baptist's head on a banquet platter (Mark 6:14-28).

Horrifying.

So, how did both the religious leaders and their irreligious king get lumped into the same warning from Jesus? Simple: they shared the same pervasive, stubborn, and abiding *un*belief.

And we're supposed to "beware of their leaven."

Leaven is a substance (typically yeast) that gets added to dough for the purpose of making it rise. The living organisms in leaven grow and spread over time, eventually affecting the entire loaf.

Like yeast, unbelief grows. It spreads, eventually affecting the entire person, sometimes even their family, circle of friends, neighbors, or co-workers. And if it sounds like we're being overly dramatic, consider some of the ways unbelief manifests itself in our current culture: the leaven of the "Me First" movement and the selfishness and entitlement it has fostered. The leaven of social media and the discontentment, disillusionment, and disconnectedness it fuels. The leaven of political obsession and the incivility and division it cultivates. The leaven of subjective truth and all the confusion and consequences it brings with it.

We could go on and on and on because there are a lot of not-great things that spread and alter and overtake. But they all begin with *not* believing what the Bible says about life and death, truth and goodness, and sin and salvation through Jesus Christ alone.

"For what can be known about God is plain to them, because God has shown it to them. For his invisible attributes, namely, his eternal power and divine nature, have been clearly perceived, ever since the creation of the world, in the things that have been made. So they are without excuse" (Romans 1:19-20).

God does not excuse our unbelief. On the contrary, He will hold us accountable for it because He has made Himself known through Jesus, the Bible, His followers, and nature itself! The Pharisees and Herod chose unbelief—in spite of every proof available to them too—because they didn't want to believe.

Indeed, they are a cautionary tale, and we mustn't be like them.

PRAYER FOCUS

Praise God for revealing Himself to you and for sending Jesus to save you and keep you (John 10:28-30). Ask God to increase your capacity to believe (Mark 9:23-24). Thank Him for being patient with you when you doubt, and for promising to give you whatever you ask according to His perfect will (John 14:13)—including, and especially, more faith to believe!

MOVING FORWARD

o   In what ways do you struggle with unbelief?

o   According to Hebrews 12:1-3, Jesus is both the founder
    (the One who establishes) and perfector (the One who
    completes) of our faith. How does that encourage you
    despite the remaining doubt or fear you may have?

o   In what ways has your faith in Jesus grown, and what
    can you do to cultivate even more?

SET YOUR MIND

Turning and seeing his disciples, he rebuked Peter
and said, "Get behind me, Satan!
For you are not setting your mind on the things of God,
but on the things of man."

MARK 8:33

There's some important context to this moment in the gospel of Mark—a solid reason Jesus referred to Peter as Satan, and here it is: Jesus was seeking God's will. Peter wasn't.

How many times have you been like Peter? The answer we all have in common is *many, many times.* Because the truth is, even in our well-intentioned moments, when our eyes are on the things of man they aren't on the things of God.

So, what are the things of man?

Well, everything that exists on the earth. Because when we

mis-prioritize and make worldly things more important than heavenly things, even good things can become bad things.

That's a lot of things.

For example, money is good and necessary, but to *love* money is to set our minds on the things of man. Relationships are good and necessary, but putting anyone above our relationship with God is to set our minds—our hearts—on the things of man. Proper healthcare is good and necessary, but when fear of sickness or plain 'ole vanity consumes us, we're setting our minds on the things of man.

Conversely, what are the things of God?

1. Who He is.

> "I am the Alpha and the Omega, the first and the last, the beginning and the end."
> Revelation 22:13

2. What He's done.

> "[Jesus] bore our sins in his body on the tree, that we might die to sin and live to righteousness. By his wounds you have been healed. For you were straying like sheep, but have now returned to the Shepherd and Overseer of your souls."
> 1 Peter 2:24-25

3. Where He says we're going.

> "Let not your hearts be troubled. Believe in God; believe also in me. In my Father's house are many rooms. If it were not so, would I have told you that I go to prepare a place for you? And if I go and prepare a place for you, I will come again and will take you to myself, that where I am you may be also."
>
> John 14:1-3

4. Why He created us in the first place.

> "Make a joyful noise to the Lord, all the earth! Serve the Lord with gladness! Come into his presence with singing! Know that the Lord, he is God! It is he who made us, and we are his; we are his people, and the sheep of his pasture."
>
> Psalm 100:1-3

When we make time and space for God in our daily routine, when we meditate on what He's done and seek to be part of what He's doing, and when we surrender our will in exchange for His, we begin to experience abiding satisfaction and a much deeper, truer sense of our purpose on earth.

It all starts with setting our minds on the things of God.

PRAYER FOCUS

Praise God that His ways are higher than our ways and His thoughts are higher than our thoughts (Isaiah 55:8-9). Thank Him for creating you for a higher purpose than what you tend to settle for. Ask Him to reveal any wrong priorities you may have and for help to reprioritize and set your mind on Him.

MOVING FORWARD

o   In what ways are you setting your mind on the things of man?

o   How does Mark 8:34-36 impact your priorities?

o   Choose one of God's attributes to set your mind on today and find a corresponding verse to memorize (helpful hint: Google "Bible verses on God's _____." (Fill in the blank with any awesome thing like love, patience, protection, provision, kindness—just to name a few.)

TRANSFIXED

Jesus took with him Peter and James and John,
and led them up a high mountain by themselves.
And he was transfigured before them,
and his clothes became radiant, intensely white,
as no one on earth could bleach them.

MARK 9:2-3

That's an oddly specific description of clothing. Clearly Mark was trying to use the best and clearest human terms he could think of, and it went something like this: Jesus' clothes were whiter than the whitest white we humans can imagine. So white, in fact, that no one on earth could bleach clothes to be so white. They were intensely and radiantly white.

We get it, Mark, we get it.

But what's the significance?

To be radiant is to send out light, to shine brightly, to glow. To radi*ate* is to emit light or energy in rays and waves. To be transformed is to make a dramatic change in form, appearance, or character. To be transfixed is to become motionless with wonder or astonishment.

And now we're getting somewhere because not only was Jesus the source of His own radiance, His power and perfection caused Peter, James, and John to become transfixed.

Imagine the scene. These three disciples had been selected to accompany Jesus up a hill, which might've felt like a chore. No doubt they were tired; all they'd been doing every day was walking around and ministering to people. They were also learning new and revolutionary things from Jesus, which likely caused their brains to be more exhausted than their feet. They surely missed their families, their hometowns, and their beds. And in this moment, nine of them got to make camp, rest, and regroup while the other three had to trudge up a hill. But in the end, the trip was worth it because the men got to see Jesus as He really is:

He's holy.

So often we see Jesus as only a man. And, of course, He *was* fully man.

"The Word became flesh and dwelt among us" (John 1:14).

Jesus (referred to as "The Word") was born, and He grew. He went to school, ate His mom's food, and learned His dad's craft. He experienced being sad and happy and everything in between. He knew hunger and thirst, exhaustion and grief, suffering and death.

Indeed, He was human, acquainted with us in every possible way (Isaiah 53:3).

But He was also fully God.

"In the beginning was the Word, and the Word was with God, and the Word was God. He was in the beginning with God. All things were made through him, and without him was not anything made that was made. In him was life, and the life was the light of men. …and we have seen his glory, glory as of the only Son from the Father, full of grace and truth" (John 1:1-4, 14).

On the mountain that day, Peter, James, and John got to see the Word in all His radiant glory—which, apart from Mark's attempt to describe it, is nearly impossible for our minds to comprehend. (Remember, think whiter than the whitest white!)

But we must try to comprehend it because knowing Jesus means knowing *all* of Him. To not only feel connected to His humanity, but to also have deep reverence for His holiness. His other worldliness. His power and position over all things, and His perfection. He is the Word who became flesh to dwell among us and save us, and we are to be His chosen people, wholly transfixed by all of who He is.

PRAYER FOCUS

Close your eyes and open your hands in a humble posture before the Lord. Praise Him because He's holy and because all things came into being through Him. Meditate on His radiance and ask God to increase your understanding and awe of who Jesus really is: fully human and fully God.

MOVING FORWARD

o   Why is this story important for you to know?

o   According to John 1:1-17, why did Jesus (the Word) become flesh?

o   In what ways do you need to adjust your understanding of who He really is?

THICK

[Jesus] was teaching his disciples, saying to them,
"The Son of Man is going to be delivered into the hands
of men, and they will kill him. And when he is killed,
after three days he will rise."
But they did not understand the saying,
and were afraid to ask him.

MARK 9:31-32

It makes perfect sense that the disciples were afraid to ask Jesus what He meant. After all, it was terrible news that was antithetical to everything they were taught the Messiah would be and do.

"Son of Man" was the Old Testament title for the Messiah, the One who would rescue the nation of Israel and permanently reign (Daniel 7:13-14). Which means Jesus' followers were fully aware of the claim He was making when He referred to Himself that way. They did, in fact, believe He was the long-awaited Savior of the world.

So then, why did the disciples not understand the rest of what He was saying?

Well, because they were a little thick in the head.

Incidentally, so are we.

The guys had all the information. They knew Jesus was the Son of Man (i.e., the Son of God, the Messiah, and the Savior of the world [Matthew 16:13-16]). They knew He'd been saying and doing things that were upsetting the religious leaders (Matthew 12:1-8, Mark 6:6-11, Luke 20:19-26). They knew that under Jewish Law, claiming to be God was punishable by death (Leviticus 24:16, Matthew 26:63-68). And they knew John the Baptist had recently been arrested and beheaded for far less (Mark 6:14-29).

Unfortunately, the disciples' expectations for how things would go, along with their desires for what the Christian life should be like, were contrary to Jesus': "For I have come down from heaven not to do my will but to do the will of him who sent me" (John 6:38 NIV).

To do God's will means to surrender our own. To spend time with God, reading our Bibles and listening closely for what His will actually is. To intentionally open our minds and hearts to whatever He wants us to understand. To let go of our personal expectations and desires. To go and do and be whatever He wants us to go and do and be.

In a nutshell, God's will for Jesus was to seek and save lost people. And for that, the Son of Man would be delivered into the hands of men to be tortured and killed. And then He would rise from the dead, defeating sin and death in the process. *That* was the plan He was sharing with His followers, and He was singularly focused on His mission.

Incidentally, so should we be.

Of course, it takes courage to not be thick in the head, to seek understanding, and to follow Jesus wherever He leads. But oh, that we'd adjust our expectations and lay down our personal desires in order to embrace His. Because, just as the disciples eventually discovered, therein lies *our* true purpose and the will of the One we follow:

To seek and save the lost, no matter the personal cost.

PRAYER FOCUS

Praise Jesus for seeking and saving you. Meditate on His extraordinary love (Ephesians 3:14-19) and the lengths He has gone to in order to save lost souls (Isaiah 53:5). Ask Him for a greater understanding of His Word, discernment to know His will, and courage to participate in His mission.

MOVING FORWARD

o   Are there things about Jesus or His will for your life that you don't want to understand?

o How does Ephesians 3:14-19 make you feel, and what does it make you want to do? (If you don't have an answer to that question, ask God for some ideas: "Lord, help me know how to respond to your love today.")

o Who in your life needs to know what Jesus did so they could be saved?

~~WHAT~~ WHO HAS YOUR HEART?

Jesus, looking at him, loved him, and said to him,
"You lack one thing:
go, sell all that you have and give to the poor,
and you will have treasure in heaven;
and come, follow me."

MARK 10:21

Unlike this new guy, the disciples weren't required to sell everything they owned prior to following Jesus. Maybe that was because they didn't have much to sell. Or maybe there was more to this moment than meets the eye.

Jesus and His followers were embarking on another walk-about when a very wealthy man approached. "Good Teacher, what must I do to inherit eternal life?" Interesting choice of words. Of course, lots of people were asking similar questions of Jesus, but a key to understanding this man might've been his use of the word *inherit* (v. 17), which means "to receive, to get, to come into possession of." No doubt he possessed a lot of things—an inheritance he'd already received or that his children would receive.

Either way, inheritance was on his mind.

The rich man also called Jesus "good," and of course Jesus *was* good. But seizing on that particular word, Jesus said, "Why do you call me good? No one is good except God alone" (v. 18). In other words, "Are you calling me God? In which case, are you willing to trust me and do what I say, no matter *what* I say? Ok then, let go of your money—your stability, your plans, your earthly inheritance—and follow me."

And now we're getting to it. Because Jesus knew the one thing keeping this otherwise sincere man from *truly* following was his money. "Disheartened by [what Jesus said, the man] went away sorrowful, for he had great possessions" (v. 22).

Money had his heart, which is why he went away sad. He wanted to follow Jesus, but he wanted his lifestyle more. And in our honest moments, we have to admit we're a lot like him—that there are things in our lives that sometimes eclipse our love for Jesus. Things that, if it came right down to it, we'd choose over God Himself.

Are you in a relationship the Lord is asking you to leave behind? Are you attending a school or working a job or living in a place He doesn't want you to be? Are you clinging to a dream that doesn't align with His plans for your life? Are you hoarding your time or treasure while He's prompting you to give more of it away?

What or who has your heart instead of Jesus?

The saddest thing about this story isn't the man's choice to walk away, though that part is indeed sad. The saddest thing is the way Jesus looked at him when he did.

"And Jesus, looking at him, loved him" (v. 21).

Our hearts were made to know and love and *be loved* by Jesus. Which means choosing anything over Him will ultimately leave us sad. But oh, that we'd believe His ways are better than ours (Isaiah 55:8-9). Oh, that we'd trust His promise to provide everything we truly need (Philippians 4:19). And oh, that we'd turn our eyes toward heaven where real treasure awaits (Matthew 6:19-21).

Oh, that Jesus would have our hearts.

PRAYER FOCUS

Praise Jesus for loving you and inviting you to follow Him with your whole heart. Hold out open hands to the Lord and confess the things that are competing with your love for Him. Ask for wisdom to know what needs to change in your life, and for humility, strength, and courage to truly follow.

MOVING FORWARD

o   What's keeping you from following Jesus wherever, whenever, or however He leads?

o   How does Isaiah 55:8-9 speak to your priorities or fears?

o   What promise does Jesus make in Mark 10:29-30 to those who choose Him above all else?

THE LUKE SERIES

(Who the heck is Luke?)

Also not a member of the twelve apostles, Luke is the author of the third New Testament Gospel and also the Book of Acts, which are the longest books of the New Testament. In fact, Luke contributed more to the New Testament than any other writer, including the apostle Paul.

He is traditionally held to be the apostle Paul's fellow worker (Philemon 24) and devoted friend (2 Timothy 4:11), as well as the "beloved doctor" (Colossians 4:14). In addition to calling Luke a physician, Paul indicates he was a Gentile, making him the only non-Jewish author in the entire Bible.

There is a long-standing, extra-biblical tradition that Luke was an artistic painter, and some ancient paintings have been attributed to his hand. He has been honored as the patron saint not only of physicians but also of artists, magistrates, and notaries.

DAY 15

A PETITION AGAINST PRESUMPTION PART 1

"I did not presume to come to you.
But say the word, and let my servant be healed."

Luke 7:7

Presumption can be hard to detect at first because, like faith, it requires a certain amount of audacity. But it's the wrong kind of audacity. Presumption is that gross, unwarranted boldness that oozes from those who think rules are for chumps, and God's authority is up for interpretation.

Simply put, presumption refuses to believe God.

The Israelites were often the poster children for

presumption. During one of their many rebellious fits, they took it upon themselves to fight the Amalekites after God had explicitly warned them not to. Through Moses, God said: (1) I will *not* be with you. (2) You will *not* win. (3) You *will* fall by the sword. (See Numbers 14:41-43.)

Although God's authority couldn't have been clearer, they chose to go with their own interpretation. "Nevertheless, in their *presumption* they went up toward the highest point in the hill country, though neither Moses nor the ark of the Lord's covenant moved from the camp" (Numbers 14:44 NIV).

The Israelites dove headlong into a battle with the most unwarranted boldness ever. Not only was it unbelievably stupid, but the fight was terribly costly. "The Amalekites and the Canaanites who lived in that hill country came down and attacked them and beat them down all the way to Hormah" (v. 45 NIV)—which was a very long way, and many men fell by the sword.

Their gross presumption explains why God asked Moses earlier in the chapter, "How long will these people treat me with contempt? How long will they refuse to believe in me, in spite of all the signs I have performed among them?" (v. 11 NIV)

Simply put, God refuses to accommodate presumption.

Now, compare that to the Roman centurion who sought healing for his servant. Because he had a healthy respect for rules and understood the mechanics of authority, he didn't presume an audience with Jesus. He saw the signs Jesus performed; he believed His words, and with the right kind of audacity he humbly asked, "I did not presume to come to you. But say the word, and my servant will be healed" (Luke 7:7).

The woman who reached for the hem of Jesus' garment displayed a similar kind of boldness (Mark 5:25-34). So did the Canaanite woman who pleaded with Jesus to heal her daughter. Afterward Jesus said to her, "It is not right to take the children's bread and throw it to the dogs." She said, "Yes, Lord, yet even the dogs eat the crumbs that fall from their masters' table" (Matthew 15:26-27).

There wasn't a trace of presumption in her request. She, too, understood the rules and audaciously petitioned Jesus for an exception. Jesus responded to her humility by saying, "Woman, you have great faith! Your request is granted" (v. 28 NIV).

Simply put, God refuses to ignore bold faith.

Since presumption can be confused for faith, we must examine the origin of our audacity. If we're diving headlong into battles with unwarranted boldness, we must know that our refusal to believe God is not going to end well. But if we have a healthy respect for the rules and God's authority, then we can boldly ask Him to "say the word," and our faith will not be ignored.

PRAYER FOCUS

Praise God for both His rules and His authority. Ask Him to reveal the ways in which you've been the poster child for presumption. Thank Him for allowing you to boldly approach His throne and ask anything in His name.

MOVING FORWARD

o   Has there been a time when you thought you were being bold in your faith but realized it was actually presumption? What was the circumstance? What was the outcome?

o   Read Numbers 14. What did Moses say to the rebellious Israelites in verse 41?

o   What request would you audaciously yet humbly like ask Jesus?

A PETITION AGAINST PRESUMPTION PART 2

During the days of Jesus' life on earth, he offered up prayers and petitions with fervent cries and tears to the one who could save him from death, and he was heard because of his reverent submission.

HEBREWS 5:7 NIV

What life-changing endeavor are you pursuing right now? Raising a family? Building a business? Earning a degree? Destroying a people? Saving a people? You can assess whether or not your effort is presumptuous by how much you pray. If it necessitates continually petitioning God for His supernatural direction, provision, timing, and favor, then you're probably on the right track. If it hasn't required any prayer at all, welllll… you might want to pray about that.

Jesus fervently petitioned the Father on a regular basis. Many of us are familiar with the blood-sweating, garden of Gethsemane prayer, but that wasn't the only time He tearfully cried out to God. The author of Hebrews informs us that it was during the days of His life. *Days.* Plural. Which means Jesus' endeavor to save His people required continuous submission to His Father's authority.

There's an Old Testament queen who understood the necessity of reverence when petitioning authority for help. Her life literally depended on it. Husband or not, approaching the king without being summoned was an automatic death sentence—unless he deemed otherwise. That notwithstanding, Queen Esther took the risk because of what was on the line.

She'd been informed of a diabolical plan to annihilate the entire Jewish population. Haman, the genocidal maniac who concocted the whole thing, did so with relative ease due to his close connection to the king. Lies were told. An edict was made. And the Jews were irrevocably doomed.

Until Esther. Her life-saving endeavor was initiated by three full days of fasting and prayer by Esther and all the Jewish people. That's a lot of prayer. Then she bravely approached the king who generously allowed her to live. That's a lot of favor. A few wine-flowing banquets later, the king asked Esther, "Now what is your *petition*? It will be given you. And what is your request? Even up to half the kingdom, it will be granted" (Esther 5:6 NIV). That's a lot of provision.

Esther brought up the edict, her doomed people, and the lies that were told. "[The king] asked Queen Esther, 'Who is he, and where is he, who would *presume* to do such a thing?'" (7:5 NASB) And then, Haman was exposed for being the presumptuous genocidal maniac that he was, right before he was sentenced to being empaled on a giant pole. The truth was told. A new edict was made. And the Jews were irrevocably rescued.

Despite the royal drama of it all, there's a major lesson from which we commoners can draw: presumption leads to death whereas petition leads to life.

If the King of kings fervently prayed throughout the days of His life on earth, how much more do our efforts necessitate total dependance on the Father? A lot more, as it turns out. How presumptuous of us to think otherwise.

Continually petitioning God for help is the only way for us to stay on the right track. Our lives depend on it. When we cry out to the One who can save us from death, He rewards us with His supernatural direction, provision, timing, and favor. Throughout the days of our lives, our reverent submission will lead to His irrevocable rescue. And what endeavor could be more life-changing than that?

PRAYER FOCUS

Praise God that you may approach Him and that He generously allows you to live. Offer up the prayers and petitions that are on your heart. Thank Him for hearing you and rewarding you with His supernatural direction, provision, timing, and favor.

MOVING FORWARD

o   What life-changing endeavor are you pursuing right now? Does it necessitate continually petitioning God? If yes, in what ways has He answered you?

o   Look up 1 Samuel 15:23. What is presumption compared to in that verse?

o   Look up Philippians 4:6-7. What is promised to follow our prayer and petition?

DAY 17

CURIOUS

Herod the tetrarch heard about all that was happening, and
he was perplexed, because it was said by some that John
had been raised from the dead, by some that Elijah had
appeared, and by others that one of the prophets of old had
risen. Herod said, "John I beheaded, but who is this about
whom I hear such things?" And he sought to see [Jesus].

LUKE 9:7-9

Herod was a bad dude, albeit a curious one, and he took
an interest in John the Baptist. At first, he protected the rogue
preacher because he feared his influence with the people. But he
also genuinely enjoyed listening to him speak (Mark 6:18-20).
That said, the corrupt ruler eventually had John beheaded because
curiosity wasn't enough to move Herod from bad to good. From
darkness to light. From sinner to saved.

Indeed, interest in and even positive feelings toward Jesus aren't enough to save us. It takes quite a bit more than that: "[Jesus] said to all, 'If anyone would come after me, let him deny himself and take up his cross daily and follow me. For whoever would save his life will lose it, but whoever loses his life for my sake will save it'" (Luke 9:23-24).

Following Jesus isn't a spectator sport. We actually have to go where He goes and do what He does because *following* is an action word. Incidentally, so is *believing*. Meaning, if you actually believe Jesus, your life changes course because you're following instead of leading.

And if you follow Jesus, like Him, you're gonna have to take up a cross.

Of course, most of us will never be required to carry a physical cross, though there are still plenty of martyrs for the faith. Instead, we're called to put our selfish and sinful desires to death—to deny them and live the way Jesus did: "I have been crucified with Christ. It is no longer I who live, but Christ who lives in me. And the life I now live in the flesh I live by faith in the Son of God, who loved me and gave himself for me" (Galatians 2:20).

That's a tall order, and it's the opposite of what the culture preaches. Every single day, we're told to put *ourselves* first because we deserve to be happy… and the world's brand of happiness comes by indulging ourselves, not denying ourselves.

Just like Herod.

But the self-indulgent king is a cautionary tale because he lived and died serving himself. And, of course, his curiosity died with him because curiosity isn't enough to save us. Having positive feelings toward Jesus isn't enough.

What saves us is what comes after.

Do you believe Jesus is the Son of God, Redeemer, Healer, and Savior of the world? If your answer is truly yes, your belief must translate into the action of following. Into going where Jesus goes and doing what He does. Into putting your sin and selfishness to death and living for Jesus instead.

PRAYER FOCUS

Praise Jesus for taking up His cross for your sake. Thank Him for what He endured and that He wants you to walk through life with Him all the way into eternity! Pray for strength and faithfulness to take up your own cross and to faithfully follow by dying to your sin and selfishness—at the beginning of your journey with Jesus and every day after.

MOVING FORWARD

o   It's great to be curious, especially about Jesus. In what ways has your curiosity led you to Him?

o   In what ways are you still living for yourself?

o   Matthew 6:24 says, "No one can serve two masters, for either [you'll] hate the one and love the other, or

[you'll] be devoted to the one and despise the other."
What or who in your life keeps you from following and
serving Jesus with your whole heart?

COUNT THE COST

As they were going along the road,
someone said to [Jesus],
"I will follow you wherever you go."

Luke 9:57

As Christians, we spend a lot of time declaring the beauty and availability of God's grace—as well we should. We should be shouting about His free gift of salvation from the rooftops because Jesus took the penalty for our sins so that we could be forgiven, redeemed, and rewarded with eternal life in heaven.

And, once we know Him personally, we can't help but tell others about His love, forgiveness, acceptance, and power to save. Jesus is life (John 14:6) and the One in whom our hearts are made whole (Jeremiah 24:7).

All of that's true and freely offered.

But also, it costs us everything.

So, how do those ideas go together? How can something be free but also cost us everything?

Well, take a look at the early followers of Jesus. They certainly didn't earn their place in the group. On the contrary, they were hot messes, each in their own way. Simon was a rash, brash fisherman. Matthew was a thieving, indifferent-to-suffering tax collector. And Mary was possessed by seven demons. But Jesus welcomed them anyway, just as they were, because following Him is a gift freely offered.

They did, however, have to walk away from their nets and tax collection booths; they had to let go of their old lives. As they followed Jesus—as they spent time with Him, listening to Him teach and watching Him heal—they became more like Him. They became the men and women we now consider heroes of the faith.

But that *is* the catch, because in order to become like Jesus, we have to leave our old lives behind. We have to go with Him. And in this passage of Luke, Jesus is telling us to count the cost: "Jesus said to him, 'Foxes have holes, and birds of the air have nests, but the Son of Man has nowhere to lay his head'" (v. 58).

You want to follow Me? Your security will have to be in Me, not your home, your job, your bank account, or anything else that makes you feel safe.

"To another [Jesus] said, 'Follow me.' But he said, 'Lord, let me first go and bury my father.' And Jesus said to him,

'Leave the dead to bury their own dead. But as for you, go and proclaim the kingdom of God'" (vv. 59-60).

You want to follow Me? You'll have to trust My wisdom, timing, and priorities instead of your own.

"Yet another said, 'I will follow you, Lord, but let me first say farewell to those at my home.' Jesus said to him, 'No one who puts his hand to the plow and looks back is fit for the kingdom of God'" (vv. 61-62).

You want to follow Me? You'll have to put Me above everyone else. You'll have to keep your eyes on Me alone. You'll have to love Me most.

Jesus welcomes everyone, but He doesn't make us stay. Far from it. He makes sure we understand what following Him will cost, which, no doubt, is why so many don't choose to follow. Most people prefer to hang onto their lives as is, to retain whatever degree of control they think they have.

But for those of us who *do* stay—for those who spend time with Him, listening to Him teach and witnessing Him heal us and others—we become more like Him. And just like the men and women of faith who came before us, we'll experience this life and the next one the way He always intended for us to.

PRAYER FOCUS

Thank God for His grace and truth. Thank Him for inviting you to come just as you are, and for His promise to make you more like Him as you follow. Confess any fear you have about going with Him and ask for peace and courage to faithfully remain no matter the cost.

MOVING FORWARD

o   How do you feel when you read verses about the cost of following Jesus?

o   What has following Jesus cost you already?

o   What has following Jesus brought to your life? Your heart? Your security? Your choices? Your sense of belonging?

MULTIPLY

The Lord [Jesus] appointed seventy-two others and sent
them on ahead of him, two by two, into every town and
place where he himself was about to go. And he said to
them, "The harvest is plentiful, but the laborers are few.
Therefore, pray earnestly to the Lord of the harvest to send
laborers into his harvest."

Luke 10:1-2

Once again, Jesus was sending His followers ahead
to preach and heal in His name. But this time seventy-two
went, not just twelve—which is an easy passage of Scripture
to overlook. After all, we know the names of the original
disciples. We know their spiritual struggles and successes.
We know where they went on their missionary journeys after
Jesus was crucified and raised, and we even know how most of

them died. Indeed, there are songs, statues, cathedrals, even whole cities memorializing the things they did to help grow the kingdom of God.

But many lesser-known people followed Jesus too. And they brought more people to Jesus, who brought more people to Jesus, who brought even more people Jesus.

And now *you're* here, reading a book about Jesus because someone, somewhere, at some point told you about Him. That's how it works. That's the way it has always worked. The gospel of Jesus gets shared, and it spreads. Which means, our words and choices impact not only the people around us, but also history *and eternity* as well.

We go.

We tell.

We sow seeds.

We reap.

But let's back up because the seventy-two sent by Jesus were no more prepared for their two-by-two journeys than the apostles were; no one ever really is. Which is ironic, considering we often assume that in order to share Jesus, we have to have the right credentials. We think we need to have more experience. We feel pressure to have our emotional and spiritual ducks in a row before telling others about the love, help, and healing we've received from Jesus.

Doesn't sound right, though, does it?

Truth is, God doesn't need us to be more ready than we are right now. Think about it: not one of the seventy-two who were sent by Jesus was capable of miraculously healing people. They weren't equipped to answer all the hard questions they were asked. For that matter, they weren't able to handle the growing opposition from their own religious leaders, let alone Rome.

They weren't even the first followers of Jesus to be sent!

But Jesus didn't need them to be or do any of those things. *He* was capable, and it was His power and provision and purpose working through them that enabled them to carry out the work.

It's as simple as that.

The harvest is plentiful, and the laborers are too few. But as followers of Jesus, we're still called to work the field, and we mustn't wait to feel more prepared because God Himself goes with us, supplying everything we need, every moment we need it. And the people we help bring to Jesus will bring more people to Jesus, who will bring more people to Jesus, who will bring even more people to Jesus.

Because that's how it works in the Lord's field.

"God is able to make all grace abound to you, so that having all sufficiency in all things at all times, you may abound in every good work" (2 Corinthians 9:8).

PRAYER FOCUS

Praise God that someone, somewhere, at some point told you about Him. Thank God for calling you to also participate in His plan to grow His glorious kingdom. Pray for courage to go into the field, and for wisdom, words, and the spiritual work ethic you'll need once you're inside.

MOVING FORWARD

o How was the gospel of Jesus sown and reaped in your own life?

o In what ways do you feel unprepared or ill-equipped to work the field? How does 2 Corinthians 9:8 speak to those feelings?

o Who is God putting on your heart right now to share Jesus with?

WHAT'S IN A NAME?

The seventy-two returned with joy, saying, "Lord, even
the demons are subject to us in your name!" And he said
to them, "I saw Satan fall like lightning from heaven.
Behold, I have given you authority to tread on serpents
and scorpions, and over all the power of the enemy, and
nothing shall hurt you. Nevertheless, do not rejoice in this,
that the spirits are subject to you, but rejoice that your
names are written in heaven."

LUKE 10:17-20

It's not surprising that the seventy-two were pumped.
Their missionary journeys were mind-blowingly awesome.
They were healing people and exorcising demons in Jesus'
name, and in so doing, their faith in Him as the long-awaited
Messiah was 100% affirmed. This was it. They had found the

Savior of the world, and He was empowering them to restore and recruit others.

For a moment, Jesus joined in their excitement, recounting how Satan had been cast out of heaven (Isaiah 14:12) and reiterating that through Him that same power was being made available to them.

Consider that for a moment: Jesus included His followers in the work.

He still is. And to accomplish His plans, He lends us His power when and how He sees fit. Amazing, right? However, according to Jesus, even that pales in comparison to the ultimate gift: heaven itself.

"Nevertheless, do not rejoice in this… but rejoice that your names are written in heaven."

Jesus became one of us in order to make God's plan of redemption known. And, of course, He accomplished the plan by dying in our place and raising back to life, forever defeating sin and death and Satan himself. When we believe that, our names are written in the book of life.

"I saw the dead, great and small, standing before the throne, and books were opened. Then another book was opened, which is the book of life. And the dead were judged by what was written in the books, according to what they had done. And if anyone's name was not found written in the book of life, he was thrown into the lake of fire" (Revelation 20:12, 15).

Our names being written in God's book of life is the whole point of the whole thing. Because those whose names are written in the book will spend eternity with Him in heaven. Those whose names are not written in the book—those who choose to not believe and not follow Jesus—will be cast out of heaven, just like Satan was.

It's tempting to only share the good news about Jesus. To be pumped about the preaching, healing, and rescuing part. And, of course, we *should* be pumped because there's no better thing we can do with our lives than 1) to know and follow Jesus, and 2) to tell others they can too.

But we also need to understand what happens when people don't.

Jesus is life, and we are saved by His name. We are empowered to do kingdom work by His name. We are granted access to heaven by His name where we'll hear *our own names* read aloud from the book of life. And then everyone—whether they chose to follow Jesus or not—will bow to the One whose name is above every other name.

"God has highly exalted [Jesus] and bestowed on him the name that is above every name, so that at the name of Jesus every knee should bow, in heaven and on earth and under the earth, and every tongue confess that Jesus Christ is Lord, to the glory of God the Father" (Philippians 2:9-11).

PRAYER FOCUS

Praise God for the opportunity to have your name written in the book of life. Ask for His help, power, and courage to do the kingdom work He has planned and set aside for you to do. Pray for more opportunities to share the gospel with others, that they too might hear their names read aloud in heaven.

MOVING FORWARD

o   Is your name written in the book of life? Why or why not, and how can you be sure?
(Hint, hint: read 1 John 5:11-13.)

o   Isaiah 14:12 describes how Satan was cast out of heaven. According to Revelation 20:15, how is that similar to what will happen to non-believers at the end of the age?

o   Whose name is coming to your mind right now that needs to know Jesus, and what are you going to do about it?

THE GOOD SAMARITAN

Behold, a lawyer stood up to put him to the test, saying,
"Teacher, what shall I do to inherit eternal life?" [Jesus]
said to him, "What is written in the Law? How do you
read it?" And he answered, "You shall love the Lord your
God with all your heart and with all your soul and with all
your strength and with all your mind, and your neighbor
as yourself." And he said to him, "You have answered
correctly; do this, and you will live."

LUKE 10:25-28

There's a lot going on here because Jesus also said, "I
am the way, and the truth, and the life. No one comes to
the Father except through me" (John 14:6)—which means

salvation comes by faith in Jesus alone (i.e., His victory over sin and death). And yet, in this moment, Jesus responds to the man's salvation question in a way that appears to assert some additional requirements to love.

But let's back up because, in context, the wise guy asking Jesus questions was testing Him. Indeed, people were always trying to trap Jesus in His words in order to discount Him entirely. So, Jesus, being the wisest guy, responded by using the man's own measuring stick: the Law itself (i.e., the Ten Commandments).

The first commandment is, "You shall have no other gods before me," and the next three support the first—no idols, honor God's name, honor His holy day (Exodus 20: 2-11).

In other words, love God with all your heart, soul, strength, and mind.

The rest of the commandments have to do with how you treat others: honor your parents, don't murder, don't commit adultery, don't steal, don't lie, and don't covet (v. 12-17).

In other words, love your neighbor as yourself.

So, in a way, the guy was right. If he kept every commandment every day, he would inherit eternal life because he'd be perfect; he wouldn't need a Savior at all. But, in a more significant way, the guy was wrong because *no one* is capable of keeping the whole Law (i.e., perfectly loving God and neighbors), which is why the Savior came. Jesus lived a sinless life and then died in our place as an atoning sacrifice so that through faith in Him we could inherit heaven (Romans 3:24-26, James 2:10-11).

Which brings us full circle and right to moment when the man asked, "Who *is* my neighbor?" (Luke 10:29)

Sigh.

Apparently, not only are we incapable of keeping the Law, but we don't even know who we're supposed to love.

Jesus responded with the well-known parable of the Good Samaritan, and it went something like this: a man (Jewish) was traveling from Jerusalem to Jericho when he was attacked by robbers and left for dead. A religious leader (Jewish) passed by but didn't help him. A Levite (Jewish) passed by but didn't help him. Then a Samaritan (half Jewish, half Gentile, and therefore wholly despised the Jews) passed by and had compassion on the man, and bound up his wounds, and paid the price to restore him back to life (vv. 25-37).

"[Jesus asked,] 'Which of these three, do you think, proved to be a neighbor to the man?' He said, 'The one who showed him mercy.' And Jesus said to him, 'You go and do likewise'" (vv. 36-37).

Here's the point. Jesus is indeed the only way to heaven because He's the only One who loves like that. But even though sin made us His enemy, Jesus didn't pass us by; He showed mercy (i.e., the cross). He has compassion (i.e., forgiveness). He binds up our wounds (i.e., healing). He gives us new life (i.e., ongoing and forever relationship with Him).

And as His followers, we should go and do likewise.

PRAYER FOCUS

Praise Jesus for rescuing you. Confess the ways you've failed to love Him and others with your whole heart. Ask for help to be more like your Savior, the One who stopped and showed mercy and sacrificed everything for your sake.

MOVING FORWARD

o   Jesus is the Good Samaritan: the One who was despised and rejected but showed mercy anyway. What are some of the ways He's been that for you?

o   In response to Christ's love, we are to love. To what degree are you loving God with all your heart, soul, strength, and mind?

o   In response to Christ's love, we are to love. To what degree are you loving your neighbors (i.e., all people, including your enemies) as yourself?

THE GOOD PORTION

As they went on their way, Jesus entered a village. And a woman named Martha welcomed him into her house. And she had a sister called Mary, who sat at the Lord's feet and listened to his teaching. But Martha was distracted with much serving. And she went up to him and said, "Lord, do you not care that my sister has left me to serve alone? Tell her then to help me."

But the Lord answered her, "Martha, Martha, you are anxious and troubled about many things, but one thing is necessary. Mary has chosen the good portion, which will not be taken away from her."

LUKE 10:38-42

There's nothing wrong with serving. Obviously. As followers of Jesus, serving is actually one of the main things we're called to do (Matthew 20:26-28). After all, Jesus served. He welcomed people when He was tired. He continued teaching when His voice grew weak. He traveled from place to place, ministering to desperate people long after His own physical exhaustion set in. And He was patient with His disciples when they didn't understand what He was saying for the umpteenth time.

He gave and gave and gave of Himself, all the way up Calvary's hill (John 19:17).

Safe to say, no one has ever served—or ever will serve—as faithfully and fully as Jesus did. So, why did He deny Martha's request for help? No doubt there were a lot of things that needed to be done that day. Many people traveled with Jesus, not just the twelve, and twelve is already a large number to feed! There were likely villagers present too, people who were hungry and tired and hurting. Surely a number of them were thankful Martha was doing exactly what she was doing.

But Jesus cared about Martha.

And about what Martha was missing.

"Martha, you are anxious and troubled about many things, but one thing is necessary."

No doubt Martha felt Jesus' compassion in this gentle correction because He wasn't dismissing her burdens. On the contrary, He tells us to bring *all* our burdens to Him: "Come to me, all who labor and are heavy laden, and I will give you rest. Take my yoke upon you, and learn from me, for I am gentle and lowly in heart, and you will find rest for your souls. For my yoke is easy, and my burden is light" (Matthew 11:28-30).

But Martha was missing a chance to sit with Jesus. And the truth is, moments with Him are more important, more precious, more burden *relieving* than anything else we could spend our time doing—and Mary knew it. She knew that at the feet of Jesus, her weary soul would be renewed. That in that sacred place, she'd gain wisdom, clarity, peace, joy, and hope for the future. That any sacrifice made to remain would be worth it because Jesus is the One in whom our souls find rest.

He is the good portion.

For as long as we live on this earth, there will be trouble and plenty of things to keep us busy, plenty that requires our attention and increases our worry. But according to Jesus, only one thing is necessary: time with Him.

Oh, that we'd be like Mary and not miss the moment.

PRAYER FOCUS

Praise Jesus for welcoming you, for wanting to spend time with you, and for His willingness to ease your anxiety and carry your burdens. Admit to Him and to yourself how hard that is to do sometimes and pray for discernment to know when you should serve and when you need more time at Jesus' feet.

MOVING FORWARD

o   Be honest. Do you believe that time with Jesus is better
    than anything else you could do with your time?
    Why or why not?

o   Do your actions reflect what you believe?
    Why or why not?

o   Fill in the blanks with your name and read this
    sentence aloud:
    "_____, _____, you are anxious and
    troubled about many things, but only one thing is
    necessary."

ACKNOWLEDGE JESUS AS LORD

"I tell you, everyone who acknowledges me before men, the Son of Man will also acknowledge before the angel of God, but the one who denies me before men will be denied before the angels of God."

LUKE 12:8-9

We shouldn't be like demons. Obviously. Problem is, like demons, some people believe Jesus lived, died, and rose again, but still don't surrender to Him as Lord: "You believe that God is one; you do well. [But] even the demons believe—and shudder!" (James 2:19)

Of course the demons believe and shudder. They were angels with God in heaven before the creation of the world.

Which means they've seen Him up close, heard His voice, and beheld His glory. But despite it all, they rebelled against God and became His enemies (Ezekiel 28:11-19). They followed Lucifer instead of the King of kings and Lord of lords (Matthew 25:41, Revelation 19:16).

Fast forward to Jesus' ministry on earth and the exorcisms He performed, and the demons who freely admitted He was the Son of God: "When the sun was setting, all those who had any who were sick with various diseases brought them to him, and he laid his hands on every one of them and healed them. And demons also came out of many, crying, 'You are the Son of God!' But he rebuked them and would not allow them to speak, because they knew that he was the Christ" (Luke 4:40-41).

They knew His name but rejected His authority over them.

They stated His identity but didn't surrender to Him as Lord.

Truly acknowledging Jesus means we accept His authority and surrender our personal control; it means making Him Lord of our lives (i.e., Master, King, Ruler). In the context of Luke 12, Jesus was telling His disciples to confess and publicly profess His identity as the Messiah to the very men who were seeking to shut the ministry down—the very men who would soon arrest, torture, and kill Jesus for who He was claiming to be.

"When they bring you before the synagogues and the rulers and the authorities, do not be anxious about how you should defend yourself or what you should say, for the Holy Spirit will teach you in that very hour what you ought to say" (vv. 11-12).

The disciples were facing intense persecution. So, publicly acknowledging Jesus before men meant surrendering to and trusting Him as Lord. It meant bowing to His rank, obeying and following no matter the circumstances, and giving up things like self-governance and self-protection.

That's the difference between those who truly acknowledge Jesus and those who don't: they make Him Lord of their lives. When we do that, we're assured He too will acknowledge us, assuring our place with Him in heaven and making us co-heirs of all that belongs to Him: the Master, King, and Lord of life.

PRAYER FOCUS

Praise Jesus because He's the King of kings and Lord of lords! Acknowledge His authority in your life, and thank Him for being worthy of your trust and faithful to meet every need that will arise as you follow Him. Ask Him to grow your courage and resolve to stand firm, and for greater sensitivity to the Holy Spirit's guidance.

MOVING FORWARD

o Have you publicly acknowledged Jesus as Lord? Meaning, do the people in your life know you follow Him? If not, why not?

o Sometimes we acknowledge Jesus as Lord, but still try

and retain control of specific aspects of our lives (i.e., finances, health, relationships, etc.). In what areas do you still need to make Jesus your Master, King, and Ruler?

o   What details are given in Revelation 20:11-15 and 21:5-8 about when and how the Son of Man will ultimately acknowledge or deny us?

ALL KINDS OF GREED

[Jesus] said to them, "Watch out!
Be on your guard against all kinds of greed;
life does not consist in an abundance of possessions."

LUKE 12:15 NIV

If you go around demanding your fair share in life, you're bound to receive a fairly demanding life lesson. That's what happened after a man in a crowd said to Jesus, "Teacher, tell my brother to divide the inheritance with me" (v. 13 NIV).

First of all, rude. Jesus was teaching a crowd of *thousands* of people about publicly acknowledging the Son of Man and fearing the One who has authority to throw them all into hell. And somehow this guy decided that was the perfect opportunity to make the moment about him and his stupid stuff.

To be clear, he was not asking Jesus for wisdom or

guidance on the matter. He was insisting that Jesus use His authority to intimidate the brother into handing over his money. Which was already ridiculous, and then he didn't even say please.

Jesus used the interruption to warn the entire crowd. He told them to guard against all kinds of greed because life does not consist in an abundance of possessions. He then illustrated His point with a parable about a rich farmer who yielded an especially big harvest.

The farmer didn't know where to store the massive pile of surplus grain, so he decided to tear down his barns, build bigger ones, then eat, drink, and be merry. As in, hoard all the extra and serve only himself. Which happens to be the blueprint for the American dream.

"But God said to him, 'You fool! This very night your life will be demanded from you. Then who will get what you have prepared for yourself?' 'This is how it will be with whoever stores up things for themselves but is not rich toward God'" (vv. 20-21 NIV).

And that was the end of the story. Jesus segued into another topic. In all likelihood, inheritance-guy stormed off miffed that his seeming injustice resulted in nothing more than a warning against being a greedy fool.

Intrinsically, this guy represents all of us. Even if we don't go around rudely demanding our fair share, we deserve this life lesson—especially those of us who've been beguiled by the American dream or any other me-first, self-love ideology.

Hoarding the surplus is so built in to who we are that it's hard at times to unclench our fists and discern the actual problem.

The problem is this: we can't serve only ourselves and still be rich toward God. Which is why we have to watch out! And be on our guard against *all* kinds of greed.

At some point our lives will be demanded from us. In that moment, all of our stupid stuff and seeming injustices won't matter one bit. Serving ourselves and hoarding an earthly surplus will be seen for the greedy foolishness that it is. Only one kind of inheritance truly matters: the eternal kind that comes from publicly acknowledging the Son of Man and serving Him. That is what life should consist of. Because that is how we are rich toward God.

"Whatever you do, work at it with all your heart, as working for the Lord, not for human masters, since you know that you will receive an inheritance from the Lord as a reward. It is the Lord Christ you are serving" (Colossians 3:23-24 NIV).

PRAYER FOCUS

Jesus made it clear that there are all types of greed. Even if you don't consider yourself to be excessive or materialistic, ask the Lord to show you where you are storing up things for yourself. Ask Him to reveal areas in which you need to be more rich toward God. Thank Him for His provision, along with His wisdom and guidance on the matter.

MOVING FORWARD

o   Possessions-wise, what do you consider to be your
    fair share in life? Does that come from a Biblical
    perspective or me-first, self-love ideology?

o   Read the parable of the rich fool (Luke 12:13-21).
    Which verse resonates the most, and why?

o   At some point, our lives will be demanded from us,
    and we will receive the inheritance we deserve. What is
    your immediate heart response to that? Fear? Concern?
    Anticipation?

CONSIDER THE RAVENS

Jesus said to his disciples: "Therefore I tell you, do not worry about your life, what you will eat; or about your body, what you will wear. For life is more than food, and the body more than clothes. Consider the ravens: They do not sow or reap, they have no storeroom or barn: yet God feeds them. And how much more valuable you are than birds! Who of you by worrying can add a single hour to your life? Since you cannot do this very little thing, why do you worry about the rest?"

LUKE 12:22-26 NIV

The words *don't worry* are difficult to take at face value. In our western lexicon, that phrase has become little more than a friendly acknowledgement—the verbal equivalent of a thumb's up or a head nod.

"Thanks for doing that."

"Don't worry about it."

Using it in a more meaningful context seems risky. Telling a person who's discouraged or struggling not to worry could be interpreted as dismissive. Or cruel. Or just dumb. And since most of us work pretty hard at not being any of those things, we choose better words to convey our compassion.

And yet, "don't worry" is exactly what Jesus told the men who would spend the rest of their lives battling discouragement and struggling through unimaginable hardship until eventual martyrdom. Thankfully, Jesus was not like any of us.

To be sure, the desire to convey the futility of worry came from the depth of His perfect compassion. Jesus loved His disciples. He didn't want them wasting headspace considering a bunch of worst-case scenarios or what-ifs. It couldn't add so much as an hour to their lives.

Nonetheless, humans have a way of clinging to delusions of self-protection and self-sufficiency, so Jesus kindly gave them something else to consider: the ravens. If God can care for a bunch of nasty, egg-stealing, scavenger birds, how much more will He meet the needs of those who love Him and are called according to His purpose? (Romans 8:28)

Fun fact about ravens: a group of them is known by several names, none of which are flattering. Most commonly, there's an *unkindness* of ravens, along with a *treachery*, a *conspiracy*, and a *murder* of ravens. Clearly, whoever decides such things wanted everyone to know these birds are jerks. Unkind, treacherous, conspiratorial, murderous jerks.

There was a major exception, however. In the Old Testament, an unkindness of ravens kindly fed the prophet Elijah while he was on the run. He was hiding from a king who wanted him dead after hearing a prophecy he didn't like. Let's consider those ravens for a minute.

God sent Elijah to a certain ravine and said, "You will drink from the brook, and I have directed the ravens to supply you with food there" (1 Kings 17:4 NIV). Which is exactly what happened. Elijah didn't freak out and worry about how that was even possible. He obeyed and, "The ravens brought him bread and meat in the morning and bread and meat in the evening, and he drank from the brook" (v. 6 NIV).

"Thanks for doing that, God."

"Don't worry about it, Elijah."

Out of the depth of His perfect compassion, God will not only feed the nasty ravens, He will direct them to supply our needs should He be so inclined. Nothing about His provision has to be rational. Which is why there's no point in worrying about the worst-case scenarios and what-ifs. Like Elijah, we are to trust the God of the impossible.

Which means, we can take Jesus' words "don't worry" at face value. He is never dismissive or cruel or dumb. He may use the most unkind of circumstances to sustain us—He may even use total jerks—but that's only to cure us of our delusions of self-protection and self-sufficiency. Because Jesus loves His disciples, He tells us not to worry. Which is the best choice of words to convey His compassion and this extraordinary promise: we will be fed.

PRAYER FOCUS

Praise God for His miraculous provision. Thank Him for the kindness He shows even through seemingly unkind means. Ask Him to help you worry less and loosen your grip on the delusions of self-protection and self-sufficiency.

MOVING FORWARD

o   If you are struggling or discouraged, how would hearing the phrase "don't worry" make you feel? How does hearing it from Jesus make you feel?

o   Are you constantly worrying about worst-case scenarios and what-ifs? What value does that add to your life? What are some other things you should consider instead?

o   What provision and protection do you need to thank God for today? List the ways He has fed and cared for you this week.

TRUST THE FATHER

"Do not seek what you are to eat
and what you are to drink, nor be worried.
For all the nations of the world seek after these things, and
your Father knows that you need them. Instead, seek his
kingdom, and these things will be added to you."

LUKE 12:29-31

As we've been discussing, acknowledging Jesus before men means more than just saying His name: it means to follow, obey, and trust what He says because of who we've acknowledged Him to be. Jesus is Lord. He's King and sovereign over all things. Therefore, we can relax and trust Him.

Easy peasy, right?

Unfortunately, things aren't always so simple because life is hard, and most of us are prone to worry, fear, and anxiousness. We can't help it because the drama is real: money runs out, kids get sick, relationships get rocky, natural disasters ensue. And *all of it* is unpredictable and painful down here on the broken, brutal planet we live on.

So then, how do we integrate our heavenly faith with our earthly circumstances? How do we stare in the face of genuinely terrifying things while refusing to be terrified? How do we, as Simon Peter exhorted, not fear what is frightening (1 Peter 3:6)? How do we lay down our self-preserving instincts and pursuits, and chase after God's kingdom instead?

By believing the King provides, that's how.

Genuine faith in Jesus has legs; it isn't idle or contained or still. Rather, it frames and shapes and impacts everything we think and do because we're operating from a place of submission to the One we trust. And He is telling us not to worry about what we need, because 1) He already knows we need stuff, and 2) He promises to provide it. As the apostle Paul said in 2 Corinthians 9:8, "God is able to bless you abundantly, so that in all things at all times, having all that you need, you will abound in every good work" (NIV).

That's a lot of *alls* and *everys*.

God provides so that we can do the work He's calling us to do. How amazing is that? We don't have to worry about having enough food, drink, clothing, or shelter over our heads because God made us and loves us and knows exactly what we need! Instead, we're to focus on the good works in front of us that build and expand His kingdom, knowing He has promised to meet all our needs already.

God provides *so that*.

See how that works? God's provision is a means to a beautiful end. His abundant care leads to our ability to participate in the expansion of His kingdom. And we can trust Him for all of it because He's the King and He said so.

PRAYER FOCUS

Thank God for your food and clothes. Meditate on all the ways He has met your needs in the past and praise Him for promising to provide in the future. Ask Him to increase your trust in His character and words, along with your courage to participate in the good works He's calling you to.

MOVING FORWARD

o   What are the things you tend to worry about the most and why?

o   How has God provided for you in spite of your anxiety and fear?

o   As you follow Jesus today, what good kingdom work is He putting on your heart to do?

BE READY FOR THE LORD

"Stay dressed for action and keep your lamps burning, and be like men who are waiting for their master to come home from the wedding feast, so that they many open the door to him at once when he comes and knocks. Blessed are those servants whom the master finds awake when he comes."

LUKE 12:35-37

Are you awake?

Jesus told His disciples to be awake and ready for the Master, the Son of Man and Savior of the world, to return at an hour they didn't expect (v. 40). According to this passage of Scripture, those who are ready will be rewarded by the Master Himself. "Truly, I say to you, [the Master] will dress himself for service and have [his servants] recline at table, and he will come and serve them" (v. 37).

On the other hand, those who are *not* ready will be cast out. "But if the servant says to himself, 'My master is delayed in coming,' and he begins to beat the male and female servants, and to eat and drink and get drunk, the master of that servant will come when he does not expect him and at an hour he does not know, and will cut him into pieces and put him with the unfaithful" (vv. 45-46).

Sounds harsh. Incidentally, those who reduce Jesus to a kind man who said nice things clearly haven't read these verses, because they're terrifyingly clear:

Followers of Jesus should be anticipating His return.

Non-followers will be punished when He returns.

But let's back up, because before Jesus can come back, He had to leave.

The more He traveled, preached, and instructed His followers, the more Jesus said about His looming death, burial, and resurrection. He spoke in parables, but He didn't speak in code. Many times He said it plainly: "[Jesus] warned them… 'The Son of Man must suffer many things and be rejected by the elders and chief priests and the teachers of the law, and he must be killed and on the third day be raised to life'" (Luke 9:21-22 NIV). (See also Matthew 16:21, 26:2; Mark 8:31, 9:31; Luke 18:31-34, 24:7.)

Jesus made it clear He wouldn't be with His disciples forever, and He was preparing them for how to behave once

He was gone: "Be awake. Be ready. Believe Me when I tell you, I'm coming back."

And now we're all caught up because Jesus was indeed crucified (John 19) and raised from the dead (Mark 16:6, Luke 24:6-7) before ascending to heaven (Luke 24:50-53, Acts 1:9) where He currently sits at the right hand of the Father (Matthew 26:64, Mark 16:19, Luke 22:69).

All of that has happened.

What *hasn't* happened yet is the coming back part, which means the exhortation Jesus gave His disciples is for us too. And we definitely need to hear it because our tendency is to get distracted and lulled to sleep by the concerns of this world. We focus on the moment we're in, losing sight of what's to come and, instead, prioritizing things that pass away. In so doing, we squander opportunities to know Jesus on a deeper level before seeing Him face-to-face.

And I, for one, want to be ready.

"The Lord himself will come down from heaven, with a loud command, with the voice of the archangel and with the trumpet call of God, and the dead in Christ will rise first. After that, we who are still alive and are left will be caught up together with them in the clouds to meet the Lord in the air. And so we will be with the Lord forever. Therefore encourage one another with these words" (1 Thessalonians 4:16-18 NIV).

PRAYER FOCUS

Praise Jesus for His promise to return, and take us to heaven, and keep us with Him forever. Confess the things that are keeping you from living in greater anticipation of that day and ask God to help you set right priorities while you wait. Pray for the people around you as you pray for yourself, that they would intimately know the One whose return is imminent!

MOVING FORWARD

o   Are you awake?

o   What distracts you from the things of God, and what priorities should you rearrange in order to keep your eyes on Him?

o   In anticipation of His imminent return, who in your life needs to be introduced to Jesus?

THE REWARD OF HUMILITY

"All those who exalt themselves will be humbled,
and those who humble themselves will be exalted."

Luke 14:11 niv

Inherent within every cultural, political, and social organization is a well-established pecking order. The priorities may vary (popularity, wealth, skill, position, beauty, etc.), but one thing remains the same:

Someone will be at the top, and someone will be at the bottom.

In Jesus' day, it was the religious leaders who determined the order and everyone's spot therein. Per usual, the lowly were at the mercy of the prominent, and the prominent were rarely merciful. The Pharisees slammed the doors of rejection loudly and publicly to keep their privileged spaces from being wasted on those with nothing to offer.

Because the kingdom of God is antithetical to man's priorities, Jesus took issue with that. What He saw being wasted was the opportunity for folks to get low and reassess their guest lists. Consequently, He told a less-than-subtle parable in the middle of a prominent Pharisee's dinner party.

Addressing the host directly, Jesus said, "When you give a luncheon or dinner, do not invite your friends, your brothers or sisters, your relatives, or your rich neighbors; if you do, they may invite you back and so you will be repaid. But when you give a banquet, invite the poor, the crippled, the lame, the blind, and you will be blessed. Although they cannot repay you, you will be repaid at the resurrection of the righteous" (vv. 12-14 NIV).

In other words, stop doing what you do. Quit looking for the temporal payoff and think instead about the eternal one. Welcome the last-picked, bottom-dwelling losers, so you can receive the ultimate blessing and repayment:

Eternity with Jesus.

Did that particular host hear Jesus' words and take them to heart? Who knows? Probably not. There's a reason why this parable comes on the heels of Jesus' declaration that "all those who exalt themselves will be humbled, and those who humble themselves will be exalted" (v. 11 NIV).

Humility among the prominent is pretty rare.

Which is why, ultimately, this parable is both a warning and an invitation to get low for all of us, not just those at the very top. Without the humility that comes from repentance, we're incapable of taking any of Jesus' words to heart. Not only will we get sucked into the pecking orders of our day, we'll also delude ourselves into believing that popularity, wealth, skill, position, and beauty are what qualify us to occupy space. Even in the kingdom of God. That's how far self-exaltation will remove us from the truth.

In the book of Revelation, the church of Laodicea is experiencing exactly that. They are deluded by their temporal, top-of-the-pecking-order status and receive harsh criticism because of it: "You say, 'I am rich; I have acquired wealth and do not need a thing.' But you do not realize that you are wretched, pitiful, poor, blind and naked" (Revelation 3:17 NIV).

Because, of course, that's who they really are. God's kingdom is antithetical to man's priorities. It's not until we recognize our true need that everything changes. Mercifully, Jesus reminded the Laodicean church, "Those whom I love I rebuke and discipline. So be earnest and repent. Here I am! I stand at the door and knock. If anyone hears my voice and opens the door, I will come in and eat with that person, and they with me" (vv. 19-20 NIV).

That is humility's ultimate repayment and reward. The doors of rejection will never be slammed. And though we have nothing to offer, we'll be counted among the righteous and have the privilege of occupying eternal space with Jesus.

PRAYER FOCUS

Pray that the Lord's kindness would bring you to repentance. Ask Him to reveal where your priorities don't align with His. Thank Him for a bottom-side up kingdom and that He is knocking at the door of your heart.

MOVING FORWARD

o Which cultural priority do you tend to get hung-up on the most? Popularity, wealth, skill, position, or beauty? How might you view it in light of eternity?

o Are there certain words of Jesus that you have trouble hearing and taking to heart? Which ones and why?

o In your own life, how have you seen humility and repentance work together? How has it changed your priorities?

GRATITUDE

[A blind man] shouted…
"Son of David, have mercy on me!"
Jesus stopped and ordered the man to be brought to him.
When he came near, Jesus asked him,
"What do you want me to do for you?"
"Lord, I want to see," he replied.
Jesus said to him, "Receive your sight; your faith has
healed you." Immediately he received his sight and
followed Jesus, praising God. When all the people saw it,
they also praised God.

LUKE 18:40-43 NIV

You'd think that every person Jesus healed would've responded exactly like the blind man. But nope, most didn't. In the preceding chapter of Luke, there's a story involving a group of healed lepers who demonstrated the opposite response—with the exception of one guy.

"One of them, when he saw he was healed, came back, praising God in a loud voice. He threw himself at Jesus' feet and thanked him—and he was a Samaritan. Jesus asked, 'Were not all ten cleansed? Where are the other nine? Has no one returned to give praise to God except this foreigner?' Then he said to him, 'Rise and go; your faith has made you well'" (17:15-19 NIV).

The mind-blowing absurdity of this deserves our attention. Ten lepers were miraculously healed from a ghastly, incurable, quarantine-necessitated disease known for open wounds, paralysis, and body parts falling off. Ninety percent of them didn't so much as thank Jesus for putting them back together and sparing their wretched lives. They simply reentered society and went on about their business.

The audacity of which makes for quite the literal illustration:

Whether it's rotting off or beautifully restored, we humans can't help but follow our flesh and carry on as if Jesus never did a thing.

Unless, of course, our abhorrent selfishness is usurped by gratitude.

That was the case with the Samaritan leper and why he humbly threw himself at the feet of Jesus. He knew he'd been restored to life and was enormously grateful because of it.

And since gratitude for Jesus is synonymous with glorifying God, faith was possible, and salvation was made known.

Asaph, one of David's chief musicians, penned an entire Psalm on the subject. He summed it up with this verse: "The one who offers thanksgiving as his sacrifice glorifies me; to one who orders his way rightly I will show the salvation of God!" (Psalm 50:23)

The inverse of that is also true. The one who does *not* offer thanksgiving does *not* glorify God and is *not* shown salvation. That's what played out with the other nine lepers. Sure, they encountered God and were physically healed. But only the Samaritan who went back to Jesus was made spiritually well.

Same was true with the blind man.

And, hopefully, the same is true for each of us.

Their stories should prompt us to ask a few questions about our own healing, like: how often do I throw myself at the feet of Jesus and thank Him for restoring the deadly disease of my flesh? When was the last time I praised God in a loud voice for sparing my wretched life? Do I audaciously go about my business as if Jesus never did a thing?

If your answers are more in line with those of the nine lepers, then follow the lead of the blind man and call out, "Jesus, have mercy on me!" And when He does, thank Him profusely because gratitude is the only right response.

PRAYER FOCUS

Thank God for all the ways He has healed you and made you well. Praise Him for the faith you have and the people who praise God because of it. Ask Him to soften your heart so you can embrace humility and stay enormously grateful.

MOVING FORWARD

o How often do you throw yourself at the feet of Jesus and thank Him for healing the deadly disease of your flesh? If it's been a while, take some time and do it now.

o When was the last time you praised God in a loud voice for sparing your wretched life? Find time this week to blast your favorite worship music and praise God at the top of your lungs!

o Do you audaciously go about your business as if Jesus never did a thing? Fill up an entire page in your journal, jotting down all the things you are grateful for.

WHAT YOUR EYES CAN SEE

Herod had seized John and bound him and put him in prison for the sake of Herodias, his brother Philip's wife, because John had been saying to him, "It is not lawful for you to have her." And though he wanted to put him to death, he feared the people, because they held him to be a prophet. But when Herod's birthday came, the daughter of Herodias danced before the company and pleased Herod, so that he promised with an oath to give her whatever she might ask. Prompted by her mother, she said, "Give me the head of John the Baptist here on a platter." He sent and had John beheaded in the prison, and his head was brought on a platter and given to the girl, and she brought it to her mother.

MATTHEW 14:3-8, 10-11

John the Baptist definitely lived life "awake." And he spent his days trying to wake up the people around him including Israel's debaucherous king. No doubt John had a good idea of what the consequences would be—no one publicly accused Herod of breaking the law without suffering a terrible end.

John did suffer, and not just because his head was cut off. While imprisoned, John struggled with doubt and disillusionment because the Messiah he preached, the salvation he heralded, and the rescue he proclaimed was imminent didn't come for him.

At least, not in the way he wanted it to.

"When John heard in prison about the deeds of the Christ, he sent word by his disciples, and said to him, 'Are you the one who is to come, or shall we look for another?'" (Matthew 11:2-3)

In other words, *Hello?!? I'm in chains for your sake… where are you?*

While John rotted in a prison cell, you know who wasn't suffering? The evil king and his disgusting new queen. Who, by the way, was not only having a shameless public affair with her brother-in-law, but she was also raising a seductress for a daughter, teaching her how to wield power and position in sinful ways. And, for all intents and purposes, the royal blended family got away with all of it. John was silenced, and the rest of the kingdom learned they better be too.

We don't know anything more about the romantic adventures of Herod and Herodias, but it's safe to say they didn't struggle like their underlings did. They lived out their days in a palace, surrounded by soldiers and servants who took care of all their needs. And isn't that often the way? Evil people prosper while "good" people don't. Of course, the Bible says there is no one good, no not one (Romans 3:10), but you get the idea. Sometimes undeserving people appear to do just fine while the godly suffer.

Which brings us back to John's jail cell because Jesus responded to His beloved servant's crisis of faith in a way that should radically change the way we see things. "Go and tell John what you hear and see: the blind receive their sight and the lame walk, lepers are cleansed and the deaf hear, and the dead are raised up, and the poor have good news preached to them. *And blessed is the one who is not offended by me*" (Matthew 11:4-6).

In other words, *you're looking in the wrong direction*.

Jesus wasn't offended by John's doubt. Instead, He reminded the Baptizer what his eyes had seen, his ears had heard, and his heart knew to be true: Messiah Jesus was indeed saving and rescuing desperate people, just like John said he would. It didn't matter that the wicked hadn't yet been punished; the Bible promises they will be in God's wisdom and at the proper time (2 Thessalonians 1:5-10). And while painful, John's suffering was not a measure of Jesus' legitimacy or even of His love for John.

So, just as Jesus chooses not to take offense, so should you not take offense when He doesn't act according to your expectations. He is not oblivious or apathetic when you struggle. He's not unaware of or absent from what you're enduring. On the contrary—He sees you and knows all things, He loves you, and He's working for your good and His glory (Romans 8:28).

And, just like John the Baptist, if you look in the right places, you'll see it too.

PRAYER FOCUS

Praise God for His constant and clearly visible work in your life and in the lives of people around you. Be specific in your prayers about the things you see and hear Him doing. Thank Him for His faithful presence and unfailing plans on your behalf. Ask Him to help you not take offense and confess and release the expectations you're still holding on to.

MOVING FORWARD

o   What are some of your expectations of Jesus? (It's not bad to have expectations…it's just not helpful to cling to them.)

o   In what ways have you seen clear evidence of His presence and power in the lives of others?

o   Hold your hands open to God in a posture of faith. Name the expectations you have and release them to Him, trusting His wisdom and timing are perfect.

BINDING AND LOOSING

Simon Peter replied, "You are the Christ, the Son of the living God." And Jesus answered him, "Blessed are you, Simon Bar-Jonah! For flesh and blood has not revealed this to you, but my Father who is in heaven. And I tell you, you are Peter, and on this rock I will build my church, and the gates of hell shall not prevail against it. I will give you the keys of the kingdom of heaven, and whatever you bind on earth shall be bound in heaven, and whatever you loose on earth shall be loosed in heaven."

MATTHEW 16:16-19

Jesus mentioned the concept of binding and loosing without explaining what it meant. That's because He didn't need to. Unlike us, the disciples weren't confused by the figure of speech. Binding and loosing was a common Jewish idiom used in regard to the Law.

To *bind* means to forbid. As in, here are all the things you *can't* do because the law says no. To *loose* means to allow. As in, here are the things you *can* do because the law says yes.

Only those with authority could go around binding and loosing, which is why the religious leaders loved it so much. It afforded them endless opportunities to flex their Torah knowledge while maintaining dominance. Their snobbery wasn't the worst of it, however. Far more egregious were the extra laws they decided to tack onto God's Law. But there's a massive difference between relaying what God has already determined and deciding it for Him.

When Jesus told His disciples to bind and loose on earth, He was revealing the kind of authority He was giving them— the kind that could unlock the kingdom of heaven and prevail against the gates of hell. It had nothing to do with maintaining dominance and everything to do with following Christ.

Which explains why the first mention of binding and loosing was immediately after Peter identified Jesus as the Messiah. Jesus told Peter that he was blessed because that revelation came directly from His Father in heaven…just like the authority to bind and loose. Every bit of it would come from God, through the Holy Spirit, because of the finished work of Christ.

In other words, it wasn't up to the disciples to decide

God's will. Or to tack on any extra requirements. The disciples were authorized to build the church, share the Gospel, and bind and loose according to the New Covenant promises.

And so are we.

To *bind* still means to forbid, and to *loose* still means to allow. But the application has changed. It's no longer a message of yes and no in regard to the Law. It's a matter of saying "yes" and "Amen" to Jesus, which means "let it be so."

Paul put it this way: "As surely as God is faithful, our message to you is not 'Yes' and 'No.' For the Son of God, Jesus Christ, who was preached among you by us… was not 'Yes' and 'No,' but in him it has always been 'Yes.' For no matter how many promises God has made, they are 'Yes' in Christ. And so through him the 'Amen' is spoken by us to the glory of God" (2 Corinthians 1:18-20 NIV).

Anyone with authority can go around binding and loosing because it's a matter of relaying God's will, not deciding it for Him. Which is exactly why the enemy hates it so much. It denies him the opportunity to flex his deception and maintain dominance in a believer's life. The gates of hell simply cannot prevail against what has already been determined in heaven.

That is the authority we have in Christ:

To declare His finished work, speak the "Amen," and let it be so.

PRAYER FOCUS

Praise God that the gates of hell cannot prevail against what has already been determined in heaven. Thank Him for the authority He has given you, through Christ, to relay His written will. Ask Him to reveal any hidden areas where you struggle to say "Amen."

MOVING FORWARD

o   Read through the first chapter of 2 Corinthians. What are the promises that are "yes" in Christ?

o   Is it easier to fixate on what you can and cannot do, rather than explore the authority you have in Christ?

o   In what area of your life do you still need to say "Amen" to Jesus? Let it be so.

THAT WHICH
MUST DIE

From that time on Jesus began to explain to his disciples
that he must go to Jerusalem and suffer many things at
the hands of the elders, the chief priests and the teachers
of the law, and that he must be killed and on the third day
be raised to life.

MATTHEW 16:21 NIV

Immediately after Peter identified Jesus as the Messiah,
Jesus explained that suffering and death would play a decisive
role in His life's work. But the disciples couldn't grasp it. Not
even a little bit. So, they opted to change the narrative because
the idea of *saving* Jesus was a lot more comfortable than
believing Him.

In true Peter fashion, he spoke the first thought that came to mind, "Never, Lord! This shall never happen to you!" (v. 22 NIV) For which Jesus cut him zero slack. He didn't respond with something like, "Oh Peter, that's sweet. I *do* have to die, but I appreciate the concern—it's the thought that counts." Jesus didn't say that because Peter's thought didn't count. For anything.

Peter's response was neither protective nor endearing. It was faithless. And for that reason, Jesus spoke rather harshly, directly addressing the one from whom the thought originated. "Get behind me, Satan! You are a stumbling block to me; you do not have in mind the concerns of God, but merely human concerns" (v. 23 NIV).

Peter wasn't reprimanded for wanting his Teacher to live. He was rebuked for supposing he could thwart the Messiah's death. The audacity of which was as self-serving as Peter's mere human concerns toward suffering in general. (Cock-a-doodle-doo.)

That was the stumbling block: their lack of faith in Jesus' work. If His disciples refused to accept the must-be-killed part, then they couldn't participate in the raised-to-life promise. One necessitates the other; both of which are the concerns of God.

That's how it works: raised-to-life promises always follow death. It's why Jesus continued with, "Whoever wants to be my disciple must deny themselves and take up their cross and follow me. For whoever wants to save their life will lose it, but whoever loses their life for me will find it" (vv. 24-25 NIV).

The disciples couldn't comprehend that yet because it's impossible to take up a metaphorical cross without the revelation of the literal one. But once they understood, once they bore witness to the resurrected Christ, it became crystal clear that suffering and death must play a decisive role in the life of each and every disciple.

With a mind renewed with the concerns of God, Peter changed his narrative. The idea of a *saving* Jesus was far more beautiful than a *comfortable* one. Decades later, in true Peter fashion, he wrote this to the persecuted church, "'He himself bore our sins' in his body on the cross, so that we might die to sins and live for righteousness; 'by his wounds you have been healed'" (1 Peter 2:24 NIV).

This time, Peter's words did count. For everything. Because he was directly quoting the One from whom they originated. In losing his life for Christ, he found it, and then dedicated himself fully to sharing the revelation of the literal cross.

PRAYER FOCUS

Praise God that Jesus suffered and died so that we may live for righteousness. Thank Him that by His wounds you have been healed. Ask Him to help you deny yourself and take up your cross in order to follow Him more closely.

MOVING FORWARD

o Is the idea of saving Jesus more comfortable than believing Him? In other words, do you ever feel the need to rewrite the narrative because you don't like something that Jesus said?

o In your own life, how have you taken up your cross and followed Christ?

o Most of the time would you say that you have in mind the concerns of God or merely human concerns? Explain.

THE IN-BETWEEN

[Jesus] cried out with a loud voice, "Lazarus, come out." The
man who had died came out, his hands and feet bound
with linen strips, and his face wrapped with a cloth.
Jesus said to them, "Unbind him, and let him go."

JOHN 11:43-44

The story of Mary, Martha, and their brother Lazarus
has massive significance, and not just because Jesus brought
a dead man back to life. Lazarus had been gravely ill, and his
sisters sent word to Jesus—who decided *not* to return in time
to heal his friend. By the time Jesus did go back, Lazarus had
been dead four days. The community, along with Mary and
Martha, were grieving, but Jesus told them to reopen the
tomb and commanded Lazarus to come out.

And then he did.

The obvious takeaway is that Jesus has power over life and death. He *is* life and gives life—physically, in the case of Lazarus, but also spiritually. When we surrender to Jesus, we're "born again;" our sins forgiven and forgotten, and we're made new. But there's a second extraordinary aspect of this famous story because before Jesus raised Lazarus from the dead, He wept.

"When Mary came to where Jesus was and saw him, she fell at his feet, saying to him, 'Lord, if you had been here, my brother would not have died.' When Jesus saw her weeping, and the Jews who had come with her also weeping, he was deeply moved in his spirit and greatly troubled. And he said, 'Where have you laid him?' They said to him, 'Lord, come and see.' Jesus wept" (vv. 32-35).

Jesus didn't weep for Lazarus. He knew His friend was about to walk out of the tomb. The circumstances were, in fact, part of a divine master plan to prove to the people watching that Jesus was the Messiah they'd been waiting for.

Which means Jesus wept because the people He loved were weeping.

Unlike Jesus, Mary and Martha didn't know their brother would be raised. They were in between—that part of the story where 1) they knew and loved Jesus, but 2) their circumstances were still overwhelming. Not only had they lost a loved one, but they'd also lost their provider and protector. Women in ancient times wholly depended on the men in their lives (their fathers or husbands or, in the absence of both, their brothers) for the very roofs over their heads. Which meant these women were not only devastated by their loss, but they were also afraid.

To add insult to their injured hearts, their Messiah, *who was also their friend*, didn't come to their rescue. At least not in the way they asked Him to, which may be why Mary didn't immediately go to Jesus when He arrived; she stayed inside. When she did speak to Him, she blamed Him. "Lord, if you had been here, my brother would not have died" (v. 32).

Jesus wasn't mad at Mary for being overwhelmed with grief and fear. And anger. He knew she was in the in-between, stuck in hard circumstances, the future unknown to her.

It was, in fact, her grief that made Him grieve—because He was in the in-between with her. That space between calling Jesus "Lord" for the first time and being delivered from the broken, brutal world we live in. That space where even though we've put our faith in Jesus, heartache, pain, and confusion still weigh heavy. That space where the way forward is sometimes unsure, and circumstances can cause us to lose sight of what's true.

But Jesus doesn't lose sight.

He knows the things you don't know.

He grieves with you as you grieve.

And He will see you through the in-between.

PRAYER FOCUS

Meditate on Christ's power over all things including life and death. Acknowledge that His ways are not your ways, and His thoughts are not your thoughts (Isaiah 55:8-9) but thank Him that He remains with you while you wait for understanding. Pour out any confusion, grief, or anger to Him in prayer. He can take it, and He loves you anyway.

MOVING FORWARD

o   Even when you follow Jesus, not everything gets resolved immediately or the way you want it to. In what ways are you in the in-between?

o   What does it mean to your circumstances—to your heart—that Jesus wept because the people He loved were weeping?

o   Read Psalm 34:18, Zephaniah 3:17, and Romans 8:28. That's all. Just read them.

OUT OF ASHES

"The Spirit of the Lord GOD is upon me, because the LORD has anointed me to bring good news to the poor; he has sent me to bind up the brokenhearted…to comfort all who mourn; to grant to those who mourn in Zion—to give them a beautiful headdress instead of ashes, the oil of gladness instead of mourning, the garment of praise instead of a faint spirit; that they may be called oaks of righteousness, the planting of the LORD, that he may be glorified."

ISAIAH 61:1-3

Through the Old Testament prophet Isaiah, God promised that the Spirit-anointed Messiah would turn sorrow into rejoicing. But what does that even mean since we know He doesn't always prevent or remove the cause(s) of our sorrow?

There are simply so many reasons to grieve. Sometimes poverty or persecution can lead us to grief. Sickness and death do for sure, not to mention coming face-to-face with our own sinfulness. As we saw in the story about Mary, Martha, and their brother Lazarus, Jesus grieves too. In fact, in Isaiah 53, He's referred to as "a man of sorrows and acquainted with grief, and as one from whom men hide their faces he was despised, and we esteemed him not" (v. 3).

It's not often we think of Jesus as a man of sorrow. In fact, when life goes into the proverbial ditch, we tend to feel like God has done something *to us*, which means we miss entirely that He's grieving *with us*. While it's true that He's sovereign (has supreme and ultimate power) and sometimes allows hard things, it's also true that He remains present in the hard things—and that He's been *through* the hard things.

Jesus lost people He loved to sickness and death too, including His cousin John the Baptist and His earthly father. He lost His reputation in His hometown of Nazareth, probably along with a lot of His childhood friends. (See Luke 4:16-29 where Jesus reads our verse of the day from Isaiah and claims to be its fulfillment!) His entire life, He was plain and overlooked (Isaiah 53:2). He was poor, so He experienced the physical discomfort of hunger pains and sleeping on the ground (Luke 2:6-7, 2 Corinthians 8:9, Hebrews 4:14-15). He was rejected, betrayed, cast aside, misunderstood, mistreated, and ultimately murdered by the very people He came to save (John 19:1-30).

He was indeed a man of sorrows, intimately acquainted with grief.

Including yours.

God sees you. He knows what grieves you, and He is grieving with you. He grieves your grief, the loss of creation as He intended it to be, and the unending ripple effects of a world that's been broken, twisted, and darkened. And He's offering Himself to you in the midst of your heartache. Think about that: the Creator of the universe, the all-powerful King, the Redeemer, and Re-Creator sees *you*. And He sees what pains you.

He's not asking you to move on from your grief more quickly. He's not impatient with you or disappointed in your inability to be okay. He knows that with some forms of pain come scars of the past and fear of the future, and He's not responding to your uncertainty by pulling away. Like any good parent responds to a hurting child, God moves toward you in your pain.

And the knowledge of that should change everything. We grieve, but God grieves with us; we are never alone. God sees us, intimately understands us, and moves toward us, never abandoning us to our pain. On the contrary, He holds us with a steadfast love and promises to bring beauty from the ashes.

PRAYER FOCUS

Sometimes we don't have words—and that's ok. If need be, just sit with God in stillness, holding your pain and heartache up to Him with outstretched arms.

MOVING FORWARD

o   What grieves you?

o   How does the grief Jesus experienced impact the way you see your own?

o   Reread Isaiah 61:1-3. Messiah Jesus came to bind up the brokenhearted and comfort those who mourn. How does that make you feel?

OFFERING

Six days before the Passover, Jesus came to Bethany,
where Lazarus was, whom Jesus had raised from the dead.
So they gave a dinner for him there. Martha served, and
Lazarus was one of those reclining with him at table. Mary
therefore took a pound of expensive [perfume] made from
pure nard, and anointed the feet of Jesus and wiped his
feet with her hair.

JOHN 12:1-3

It was a familiar scene. Jesus was hanging out with His
followers around a dinner table. Precious, hard-working
Martha was serving. And Mary was staying close to Jesus.
Only this time, her love for her Savior—for her brother's
Savior from an actual tomb—was overflowing.

Literally.

149

And just in case the significance of this moment is lost in translation, the washing of feet was a necessary part of ancient Israel custom because of course it was. Everyone walked everywhere in sandals on unpaved, dusty roads. Since Jesus and the disciples spent much of their time traveling from town to town, you can imagine how dirty their feet would've been.

When it came to the actual washing, the lowliest servant in the household was tasked with the job. Which means not only was Mary demonstrating her submission to Jesus by taking this humble posture, but she was also offering Him the most and best she had.

And Judas took issue with it.

"Judas Iscariot, one of his disciples (he who was about to betray [Jesus]), said, 'Why was this ointment not sold for three hundred denarii and given to the poor?' He said this, not because he cared about the poor, but because he was a thief, and having charge of the moneybag he used to help himself to what was put into it. Jesus said, 'Leave her alone, so that she may keep it for the day of my burial. For the poor you always have with you, but you do not always have me'" (vv. 4-8).

There's a lot going on there and hindsight regarding Judas is 20/20. But he wasn't totally wrong because perfume made from pure nard *was* expensive. Which means it indeed could've been sold and the money given to the poor. Or it could've been set aside and preserved for a rainy day. After all, the death of Lazarus had exposed how vulnerable Mary and

Martha were without the protection and provision of their brother.

And yet, for Mary, this moment was really simple. She was giving an offering to the One who'd given everything to her. She wasn't weighing and counting and measuring and holding; she was worshiping. And her gift flowed from open hands and a fully surrendered heart.

Of course, she didn't know what Jesus knew: that His death was imminent. But when that day came, she must've been so, so glad she hadn't withheld such a beautiful offering.

And that's the lesson for us, because far too often we don't give Jesus our best and most. We withhold when we could worship. We count the cost when we could open our hands and fully surrender our hearts. But our death is imminent too. And when that day comes and we see Jesus face-to-face, we'll be so, so glad if, like Mary, we gladly gave Him our offerings.

PRAYER FOCUS

Pour out your heart to God in prayer. Spend time contemplating His goodness and worshiping Him as Lord. Hold your hands open in a posture of surrender and praise the One who has withheld nothing from you.

MOVING FORWARD

o Serving others and giving to the poor are things Jesus did and tells His followers to do. But we're also supposed to make Him our first and best priority. What are your priorities?

o What do you want your time at the feet of Jesus each day to look like?

o What kind of offering are you feeling prompted to give Him today?

SCHOOLED BY FISH

Who makes you different from anyone else?
What do you have that you did not receive?
And if you did receive it, why do you boast
as though you did not?

1 CORINTHIANS 4:7 NIV

In all likelihood, Peter was the disciple most prone to hubris and credit-taking. His big talk and impulsive actions demonstrated entirely too much self-confidence. Years of regaling fish stories might've had something to do with that. Fish have a way of getting bigger with each retelling. And so does the teller.

Perhaps that's why Jesus chose Peter to experience all of His fish miracles. The Lord is pretty specific that way. He knows what will shake our self-confidence enough to change the narrative and shift our focus. In Peter's case, he was schooled by a bunch of fish, for which he could take absolutely no credit. As a result, he caught a series of revelations, and it was Jesus who was deservedly made bigger.

1. Jesus used fish to call Peter.

After spending an entire night at sea catching nothing, Jesus told Simon to go back out and let down his nets. Simon Peter obeyed and caught so many fish that the nets began to break. "When Simon Peter saw this, he fell at Jesus' knees and said, 'Go away from me, Lord: I am a sinful man!' Jesus said to Simon, 'Don't be afraid; from now on you will fish for people.' So they pulled their boats up on shore, left everything and followed him" (Luke 5:8, 10 NIV).

The miraculous catch of fish prompted Peter to accept his calling.

2. Jesus used fish to feed Peter.

After spending an entire day listening to Jesus preach, the disciples asked Jesus to send the crowd away so they could find food and lodging. Jesus replied, "'You give them something to eat.' They answered, 'We have only five loaves of bread and two fish—unless we go and buy food for all this crowd.' (About five thousand men were there.) But he said to his disciples, 'Have them sit down in groups of about fifty each.' The disciples did so, and everyone sat down. Taking the five loaves and the two fish and looking up at heaven, he gave thanks and broke them. Then he gave them to the disciples to distribute to the people. They all ate and were satisfied, and the disciples picked up twelve basketfuls of broken pieces that were left over" (Luke 9:13-17 NIV).

The miraculous multiplication of fish enabled Peter to feed himself and the masses.

3. Jesus used a fish to teach Peter.

After arriving in Capernaum, the collectors of the temple tax asked Peter, "'Doesn't your teacher pay the temple tax?'

'Yes, he does,' he replied" (Matthew 17:24-25 NIV).

When Peter came into the house, Jesus asked him about the tax and said to him, "So that we may not cause offense, go to the lake and throw out your line. Take the first fish you catch; open its mouth and you will find a four-drachma coin. Take it and give it to them for my tax and yours" (v. 27 NIV).

The miraculous provision in the fish taught Peter that Jesus controls everything.

4. Jesus used fish to commission Peter.

After the resurrection, Jesus appeared to His disciples by the Sea of Galilee. They'd been fishing all night, and, once again, caught nothing. Jesus called out to them, "'Friends, haven't you any fish?'

'No,' the answered.

He said, 'Throw your net on the right side of the boat and you will find some.' When they did, they were unable to haul the net in because of the large number of fish" (John 21:5-6 NIV).

As soon as Peter heard one of the other disciples exclaim,

"It is the Lord!" Peter jumped into the water and headed for shore (v. 7 NIV).

The miraculous catch of fish propelled Peter to embrace Christ's commission.

Needless to say, Peter never stopped regaling fish stories. They were too big not to tell. Each miraculous account was shared over and over, minus any hubris and credit-taking, because Peter's boast was in the Lord.

Like with Peter, Jesus will take what we do for a living and show us how to live for Him. The Lord is pretty specific that way. He knows what will shake our self-confidence enough to change the narrative and shift our focus. He will use the familiar to prompt, enable, teach, and propel us to catch a series of revelations that cause us to place our confidence in Him. And as we do, we'll boast in the only One who deserves to get bigger with each retelling of the story.

PRAYER FOCUS

Praise God for using the familiar to change your narrative and for inviting you into His story. Ask Him to prompt, enable, teach, and propel you in new ways. Thank Him for being a miracle-working God in whom you may boast.

MOVING FORWARD

o Be honest. In what areas of your life are you most
   prone to hubris and credit-taking? Is it a skill you've
   mastered or talent that comes naturally?

o With the fish miracles, Jesus eliminated any chance
   of Peter boasting in his own abilities. Have you
   experienced anything similar? As in, has the Lord
   shaken your self-confidence so you'd place your
   confidence in Him? Explain.

o What personal story do you most enjoy regaling about
   Jesus? What revelation did you catch? How did Jesus
   become bigger in your life as a result?

DAY 37

THE VALUE OF HUMILITY

Do nothing out of selfish ambition or vain conceit. Rather, in humility value others above yourselves, not looking to your own interests but each of you to the interest of the others.

PHILIPPIANS 2:3-4 NIV

The reason Paul told the church to do nothing out of selfish ambition or vain conceit is because it's our natural tendency to do everything out of either or both. Our flesh can't help but crave exaltation. And our hearts, which have been described as deceitful and beyond cure, will high-five that compulsion all day long.

Such was the case at a prominent Pharisee's house where the guests jockeyed for positions of honor around the dinner table. Before calling them out on their hunger for status, Jesus served the group some difficult questions. Although clueless as to how to answer, they were savvy enough to keep their mouths shut. Engaging with Jesus wasn't worth forfeiting their rank among men.

The obviousness of it all gave Jesus the perfect opportunity to share a parable about seating arrangements and their consequences. He said, "When someone invites you to a wedding feast, do not take the place of honor, for a person more distinguished than you may have been invited. If so, the host who invited both of you will come and say to you, 'Give this person your seat.' Then, humiliated, you will have to take the least important place. But when you are invited, take the lowest place, so that when your host comes, he will say to you, 'Friend, move up to a better place.' Then you will be honored in the presence of all the other guests. For all those who exalt themselves will be humbled, and those who humble themselves will be exalted" (Luke 14:8–11 NIV).

Needless to say, Jesus' story is more than a life hack on how to avoid embarrassment at parties. He was addressing the human compulsion to matter more than the next guy. When we're willing to take the lowest place, we recognize what actually matters *is* the next guy.

Most of us accept this intellectually but living it out is another thing entirely since "the lowest place" usually means the least glamorous seat. It's a spot at the proverbial kid's table where nary a person gathered will high-five our ambition or help advance our self-interested agendas. Which, of course, is the whole humbling point.

Instead of jockeying for positions of honor, Jesus invites us to pull up a chair next to the poor in spirit. And alongside those who mourn, the meek, and those persecuted because of righteousness. It's a personal invitation because that's the table at which Jesus sits, and His ultimate desire is that we find our place next to Him.

When we do, the promise attached is eventual exaltation—though it likely won't be the kind our flesh craves. And it may not occur this side of eternity. But there will be a day when we finally experience this revelation in full: engaging with Jesus was worth forfeiting our rank among men. In fact, it'll be worth everything we've ever had to offer because we'll hear Him say the words, "Friend, move up to the better place."

PRAYER FOCUS

Praise God for His not-so-subtle parables about our sinful condition. Thank Him for repeatedly inviting you to sit with Him in lowly places. Ask the Lord to expose and heal your deceitful heart that craves fleshly exaltation. And ask Him to show you who you can serve.

MOVING FORWARD

o Be honest with yourself. Under what circumstances
   have you jockeyed for positions of honor? As in, how
   have you tried to up your social status? In what realm
   do you find that most important? Family members,
   friend groups, work colleagues, church family, etc.?

o When we're willing to take the lowest place, we
   recognize what actually matters is the next guy. Recall
   a time when this became evident. Where were you, and
   who were you with?

o Is there something you do out of selfish ambition or
   vain conceit? How might you change your motives and
   value others above yourself? What is an action step you
   can take?

HEARD

"Go in peace, and may the God of Israel grant you what
you have asked of him."

1 Samuel 1:17 niv

We tend to label our experiences by how we feel in the moment. Which means if we are an emotional wreck, a beautiful thing can be called something terrible. On the other hand, if we have peace, then even something terrible can be considered a beautiful gift from God. It all depends on what or who is influencing our feelings.

Whichever the case, legacies are born. Stories are passed down. And generations of people are affected.

Old Testament sisters Rachel and Leah make for a good example. Through a stranger-than-fiction chain of events, the two women ended up sharing a husband and competing for his affection. The dynamic was every bit as sad and messy as it sounds. The husband, Jacob, wasn't discreet about his preference for Rachel, the beautiful though barren sister. So Leah, the "weak-eyed" unloved sister capitalized on her fertility.

After Leah's four-children-head-start, God opened Rachel's womb. Whatever gratitude Rachel felt toward the Lord was eventually usurped by the contempt she harbored toward her sister. The feeling was mutual, and their children were identified accordingly.

Leah named her first son *Reuben*, which means "See, a son!" She explained, "It is because the Lord has seen my misery. Surely my husband will love me now" (Genesis 29:32 NIV). Which seems like a lot to put on a kid.

For one of her boys, Rachel chose the name *Naphtali* because it means "my struggle." She said, "I have had a great struggle with my sister, and I have won" (Genesis 30:8 NIV).

Did she though? Rachel may have remained Jacob's favorite, but the entire household was about as acrimonious as it gets. Even the sisters' servants were given to Jacob to bear children. Who among them had an ounce of peace?

Mercifully, most of the children's names were normal, lovely even. But just because the Lord was mentioned when they were named, doesn't mean their mothers' decisions were influenced by faith. The true impetus was their bitter rivalry and desperation to win.

There's another Old Testament story with a similar

dynamic. The preferred wife, Hannah, was barren and desperately wanted children. The other wife, Peninnah, had lots of children and desperately wanted Hannah to suffer.

Despite the constant provocation and deep emotional pain, Hannah didn't fight back. Nor did she throw her status in Peninnah's face. Unlike the other women, she repeatedly brought her heartache before the Lord.

While praying in the temple one day, the priest overheard Hannah's anguish and accused her of being drunk. After Hannah explained that she was pouring her soul out to the Lord, he said, "Go in peace, and may the God of Israel grant you what you have asked of him" (1 Samuel 1:17 NIV).

Later, when Hannah gave birth to a son, she named him *Samuel*, which means "heard by God." She said, "Because I asked the Lord for him" (v. 20 NIV).

Since we tend to label our experiences by how we feel in the moment, wisdom mandates that we bring our heartache before the Lord. Repeatedly. If we don't, we may end up calling a beautiful thing something terrible like "my struggle." Then convince ourselves that we're winning when, really, our faith has been contaminated by bitterness and desperation. The outcome of which is every bit as sad and messy as it sounds.

But when we obediently bring our heartache before the Lord, even amidst constant provocation and deep emotional pain, we will go in peace. The same God of Israel who heard Hannah's anguish and gave her a son, knows the cries of our hearts, and gave us His.

Beautifully, the most terrible death in all of human history will forever be considered the ultimate gift from God. The result of which is the peace that only Jesus can give if we allow Him to fight on our behalf and influence our feelings. (See John 14:26.)

Whichever the case, legacies are born. Stories are passed down. And generations of people are affected.

PRAYER FOCUS

Praise God that He is so much bigger than your most disastrous emotions. Ask Him for the peace that surpasses understanding as you pour out your soul to Him. Thank Him for changing your legacy, your story, and the generations your decisions will affect.

MOVING FORWARD

o   Describe a time you mislabeled a situation because you were an emotional mess. From what or whom were your feelings influenced? Conversely, describe a heartrending experience in which God granted you peace after you poured out your soul to Him.

o   Read Genesis 29:31-30:24. List the names of Leah's and Rachel's children and the reasons for each.

o   Read Philippians 2:5-11. List the specific actions that caused God to exalt Jesus to the highest place and give

Him the name that is above every name. How does that change your legacy, shape your stories, and affect the generations that follow you?

PREACHING WHAT YOU PRACTICE

Don't let anyone look down on you
because you are young,
but set an example for the believers in speech,
in conduct, in love, in faith, and in purity.

1 TIMOTHY 4:12 NIV

Setting an example wasn't the only directive Paul gave his young protégé, Timothy. He also told him to ignore the criticism and get back to preaching and teaching the gospel (1 Timothy 4:13). Evidently, Timothy had slacked off from putting himself out there. He likely buckled under the scrutiny of the older down-lookers.

Because Timothy was timid in nature, fear of man was

a real issue. Which made encouragement a real necessity. In a subsequent letter, Paul reassured Timothy that fear is not from God. However, power, love, and self-control most certainly are (2 Timothy 1:7).

That truth enabled Paul to conclude his charge with this promise: "Be diligent in these matters; give yourself wholly to them, so that everyone may see your progress. Watch your life and doctrine closely. Persevere in them, because if you do, you will save both yourself and your hearers" (1 Timothy 4:15-16 NIV).

Naturally speaking, if fear-of-man was Timothy's issue, then reading the words "so that everyone may see your progress" would've been his worst nightmare. Because progress isn't perfection. Progress means mistakes. And lots of people would see those mistakes the moment he put himself out there. To that end, lots of people would be looking for those mistakes. Because that's what lots of people do.

But that didn't matter. Timothy's example wasn't contingent upon perfection. His speech, conduct, love, faith, and purity were simply the fruit of his obedience to Christ. Which means, spiritually speaking, if Timothy feared God more than man, he'd eagerly demonstrate his progress, since it was rife with power, love, and self-control.

And that's exactly what happened. After being encouraged by Paul, Timothy resumed preaching the gospel and teaching the things he'd been called to practice.

Each believer is to do likewise. Which means every last

one of us needs the same encouragement and reassurance. Because let's be real, no matter what century we live in, persevering in purity and doctrine has always invited heaps of criticism and scrutiny from the down-lookers.

But that doesn't matter. Our example isn't contingent upon the approval of others. Like Timothy, our responsibility is to practice our gifts while minding our speech, conduct, love, faith, and purity. Or as Jesus put it: letting our light shine so that others may see our good deeds and glorify our Father in heaven (Matthew 5:16).

So, if fear-of-man has been a real issue, and progressing before others your worst nightmare, be encouraged. There's no reason to slack off or buckle. The fearless Spirit we've been given is powerful, loving, and self-controlled. And it's only because of His work within us that we're able to bear fruit, set an example, and shine for Christ. To that end, lots of people have been looking for Him. They'll see Jesus more than our mistakes and glorify our Father in heaven. Because that's what lots of people do.

PRAYER FOCUS

Praise God that He uses timid, broken people like us to shine before others and bring glory to Himself. Ask Him for more power, love, and self-control so that you may set an example through your obedience. Thank Him for your continual progress.

MOVING FORWARD

o   Does setting an example in speech, conduct, love, faith, and purity seem like an impossible task?
    Why or why not?

o   In terms of living your faith out loud for others to see, what is the next right thing you can do?

o   What gifts has God given you to use for His glory?
    Does the idea of everyone seeing your progress sound like your worst nightmare?
    Why or why not?

WHAT ARE YOU WAITING FOR?

I wait for the LORD, my whole being waits,
and in his word I put my hope.

PSALM 130:5 NIV

Waiting is hard enough under normal circumstances. Waiting for something to change when life is hard can feel excruciating. David wrote about this often. In one of his psalms, after spending some time lamenting the fleeting nothingness that was the span of his years, he finally inquired of God, "And now, O Lord, for what do I wait?" (Psalm 39:7)

It's a good question. One we should ask every single day of our fleeting lives because within it contains the answer:

The Lord. We are waiting for the Lord.

To state the obvious, we wait for the Lord to change different things in different seasons. While writing that particular psalm, David was burdened over multiple issues: the prosperity of the wicked, an illness of some sort, the overall futility of life without hope in God. It was a lot. And David was spiraling. So, before receiving a perceptible answer from God, he strengthened himself with these five words: "My hope is in you" (v. 7).

David wrote about this often because it was a major theme in his life. Continually, he strengthened himself in the God who knows the purpose and outcome of each and every circumstance even the most horrific ones. Like the time when his own men plotted to stone him to death.

It happened in the town of Ziklag, David's home base during his exile from King Saul. While he and his 600 soldiers were out exterminating other enemies, the Amalekites burned Ziklag to the ground and kidnapped all of the women and children. After David and his men returned and surveyed the devastation, "[They] wept aloud until they had no strength left to weep" (1 Samuel 30:4 NIV).

Except the 600 men did manage to reserve enough strength to blame David for everything and talk of stoning him (v. 6).

Understandably, David was greatly distressed. "But [he] strengthened himself in the Lord his God" (v. 6). Moments later, David inquired of the Lord and received his perceptible answer: God told him to pursue the enemy.

With the help of divine providence and a sickly Egyptian guy, David and his men located the Amalekites, wiped them out, and rescued their women and children. Which means, not only did David's hope in the Lord give him the specific answers that he needed, it also gave him the strength to fight the enemy. David went from being too depleted to weep, to destroying the Amalekites from dusk until the evening of the next day (v. 17).

Waiting for something to change when life is hard can feel excruciating—unless we choose to wait on the Lord. That's what changes everything regardless of our season. Even if we're burdened over multiple issues and have spent time lamenting the fleeting nothingness that is the span of our years, we can strengthen ourselves with these five words:

My hope is in You.

And our faithful God, who knows the purpose and outcome of each and every circumstance, will provide a perceptible answer along with the strength to fight.

PRAYER FOCUS

Praise God that we can wait on Him and put our hope in His Word. Ask Him to strengthen you even when you feel like you are spiraling—especially when you feel like you are spiraling. Inquire of Him and listen for a perceptible answer.

MOVING FORWARD

o What hard circumstance are you waiting to change? What issues are you burdened over?

o Do you struggle to believe that God knows the purpose and outcome of each and every circumstance even the most horrific ones? Do you struggle to trust Him with each and every one?

o Today, how can you strengthen yourself in the Lord?

ABOUT THE AUTHORS

Amanda Jenkins is the lead creator for *The Chosen's* extra content. She lives in Texas with her kids and her husband, Dallas.

Kristen Hendricks writes and illustrates for *The Chosen's* extra content. She lives just outside Chicago with her husband, Joe.

Dallas Jenkins is the creator of the *The Chosen*. He lives with Amanda and his kids in Texas, where he makes *The Chosen*.

So….*The Chosen* is pretty much all they do.